Making Chicago Price Theory

Milton Friedman and George J. Stigler shaped economics as we know it today – their Chicago School laid the groundwork for much of the neo-classical tradition in economic analysis. This book brings together key letters between these two Nobel laureates from the post-war years, containing new information about their personal and professional relationships, and also illuminating the development of ideas which are now fundamental to economic theory.

The book, expertly edited by Dan and Claire Hammond, contains an introductory chapter, chronologies for Friedman and Stigler, and transcripts of 71 letters written from 1945 to 1957 along with enclosures.

J. Daniel Hammond is Hultquist Family Professor in the Department of Economics at Wake Forest University. **Claire H. Hammond** is Professor in the Department of Economics at Wake Forest University.

Routledge studies in the history of economics

Making Chicago Price Theory

Friedman–Stigler
correspondence 1945–1957

**Edited by J. Daniel Hammond and
Claire H. Hammond**

Routledge
Taylor & Francis Group

LONDON AND NEW YORK

First published 2006
by Routledge
2 Park Square, Milton Park, Abingdon, Oxon OX14 4RN

Simultaneously published in the USA and Canada
by Routledge
270 Madison Ave, New York, NY 10016

Routledge is an imprint of the Taylor & Francis Group, an informa business

Transferred to Digital Printing 2009

© 2006 Selection and editorial matter, J. Daniel Hammond and
Claire H. Hammond

Typeset in Times by Wearset Ltd, Boldon, Tyne and Wear

British Library Cataloguing in Publication Data
A catalogue record for this book is available from the British
Library

Library of Congress Cataloging in Publication Data
A catalog record for this book has been requested

ISBN10: 0-415-70078-7 (hbk)
ISBN10: 0-415-49414-1 (pbk)

ISBN13: 978-0-415-70078-8 (hbk)
ISBN13: 978-0-415-49414-4 (pbk)

Contents

George J. Stigler – Curriculum Vitae to 1958

1911	Born January 17, Renton, WA, to Joseph and Elizabeth Hungler Stigler.
1931	Received B.A. from University of Washington.
1932	Received M.B.A. from Northwestern University and enrolled in graduate economics program at University of Washington.
1933	Began graduate studies in economics at University of Chicago.
1935	Joined staff of National Resources Planning Board, Washington, DC.
1936	Joined faculty of Iowa State College, and on December 26 married Margaret Louise Mack.
1938	Received Ph.D. from University of Chicago and joined faculty of University of Minnesota.
1940	Joined staff of Defense, Defense Finance Unit, Office of Price Administration.
1941	Stephen Stigler born on August 10.
1943	Joined staff of Statistical Research Group, Columbia University. David Stigler born on August 31.
1945	Returned to University of Minnesota.
1946	Joined faculty of Brown University. Joseph Stigler born, December 2.
1947	Joined faculty of Columbia University.
1955	Sabbatical in Europe with Guggenheim Fellowship, February–July
1957–58	Sabbatical at Center for Advanced Study in Behavioral Sciences, Palo Alto, CA.
1958	Joined University of Chicago faculty as Charles R. Walgreen Distinguished Service Professor of American Institutions with joint appointment in the Graduate School of Business and Department of Economics.

Milton Friedman – Curriculum Vitae to 1958

1912	Born July 31, Brooklyn, NY, to Jeno and Sarah Landau Friedman.
1932	Received B.A. from Rutgers University and enrolled in graduate economics program at University of Chicago.
1933	Transferred to Columbia University graduate economics program.
1934	Returned to University of Chicago.
1935	Joined staff of National Resources Planning Board, Washington, DC.
1937	Joined research staff, National Bureau of Economic Research, New York City, and became part-time Lecturer in Economics Department, Columbia University.
1938	Married to Rose Director, June 25.
1940	Joined faculty of University of Wisconsin as Lecturer in Statistics with rank of Professor.
1941	Became Principal Economist, Division of Tax Research, U.S. Treasury, and Professor, U.S. Department of Agriculture Graduate School, Washington, DC.
1943	Janet Friedman born, February 26. Became Associate Director, Statistical Research Group, Columbia University.
1945	David Friedman born, February 12. Joined faculty of University of Minnesota as Associate Professor of Economics and Statistics.
1946	Joined faculty of University of Chicago.
1950	On leave fall quarter to be consultant with Economic Cooperation Administration, Paris.
1953	Year-long leave to be Fulbright Fellow at Cambridge University.
1955	On leave fall quarter to serve as adviser to Indian government under sponsorship of U.S. International Cooperation Administration.
1957–58	Sabbatical at Center for Advanced Study in Behavioral Sciences, Palo Alto, CA.

Dramatis personae

Moses Abramovitz, research staff, National Bureau of Economic Research.

Maurice Allais, Research Director, Centre National de la Recherche Scientifique.

James W. Angell, Professor of Economics, Columbia University.

Harold Barger, Professor of Economics, Columbia University.

Robert L. Bishop, Professor of Economics, Massachusetts Institute of Technology.

Francis M. Boddy, Professor of Economics, University of Minnesota.

Kenneth Boulding, Professor of Economics, Iowa State College.

Yale Brozen, Professor of Economics, Northwestern University.

Arthur F. Burns, Professor, Columbia University, Director of Research, National Bureau of Economic Research and Chairman, Council of Economic Advisers.

William J. Carson, Executive Director, National Bureau of Economic Research.

Edward H. Chamberlin, Professor of Economics, Harvard University.

[?] Cisco [unfound in sources].

Colin Clark, Economist, Queensland Bureau of Industry, Brisbane.

John M. Clark, Professor of Economics, Columbia University.

Emile Despres, Professor of Economics, Williams College.

Donald J. Dewey, Professor of Economics, Duke University.

Aaron Director, brother of Rose D. Friedman and Professor, School of Law, University of Chicago.

Evsey D. Domar, Professor of Economics, Johns Hopkins University.

Paul H. Douglas, Professor of Economics, University of Chicago.

Corwin D. Edwards, Economist, Federal Trade Commission.

Howard S. Ellis, Professor of Economics, University of California, Berkeley.

Solomon Fabricant, Professor of Economics, New York University and Director of Research, National Bureau of Economic Research.

Frank A. Fetter, Professor of Economics, Princeton University.

David Friedman, son of Rose and Milton Friedman.

Janet Friedman, daughter of Rose and Milton Friedman.

Rose Director Friedman, wife of Milton Friedman.

Sarah Landau Friedman, mother of Milton Friedman.

Thornton Fry, Acting chief, Applied Mathematics Panel, National Defense Research Committee.

John Kenneth Galbraith, Editor, *Fortune* magazine, later Professor of Economics, Harvard University.

Frederic B. Garver, Professor of Economics, University of Minnesota.

Harry D. Gideonse, President, Brooklyn College.

Richard V. Gilbert, U.S. Office of Price Administration.

Raymond W. Goldsmith, Professor of Economics, American University and research staff, National Bureau of Economic Research.

Carter Goodrich, Professor of Economics, Columbia University.

William D. Grampp, Professor of Economics, University of Illinois, Chicago.

Robert M. Haig, Professor of Economics, Columbia University.

Bernard F. Haley, Professor of Economics, Stanford University and Chairman, American Economic Association Committee on Republications.

Earl J. Hamilton, Professor of Economics, University of Chicago and Editor, *Journal of Political Economy*.

Alvin H. Hansen, Professor of Economics, Harvard University.

Charles O. Hardy, Economist and Staff Director, Joint Congressional Committee on Economic Report.

Seymour E. Harris, Professor of Economics, Harvard University.

Albert G. Hart, Professor of Economics, Columbia University.

Friedrich A. Hayek, Professor of Economics, London School of Economics.

Helene Hayek, wife of Friedrich A. Hayek.

Paul T. Homan, Professor of Economics, Cornell University, later Council of Economic Advisers. Managing Editor, *American Economic Review*.

Albert Hunold, Swiss businessman, founding member, Mont Pelerin Society.

Robert Maynard Hutchins, Chancellor, University of Chicago.

John Jewkes, Professor of Economics, Oxford University.

D. Gale Johnson, Professor of Economics, University of Chicago.

Homer Jones, Economist, Federal Reserve Board.

Carl Kaysen, Professor of Economics, Harvard University.

Frank H. Knight, Professor of Economics, University of Chicago.

Asa Knowles, Dean, School of Business, University of Rhode Island and President, Associated Colleges of Upper New York.

Andrey N. Komolgoroff, Professor of Mathematics, Moscow State University.

Richard L. Kozelka, Acting Dean, School of Business Administration, University of Minnesota.

Simon S. Kuznets, Professor of Economics, University of Pennsylvania and research staff, National Bureau of Economic Research.

Abba P. Lerner, Professor of Economics, New School for Social Research.

Richard A. Lester, Professor of Economics, Princeton University.

Edward Levi, Professor, then Dean, University of Chicago School of Law.

H. Gregg Lewis, Professor of Economics, University of Chicago.

W. Arthur Lewis, Professor of Economics, University of Manchester.

Charles E. Lindblom, Professor of Economic and Political Science, Yale University.

Erik Lundberg, Professor of Economics, Stockholm University.

Friedrich A. Lutz, Professor of Economics and Social Institutions, Princeton University.

Fritz Machlup, Professor of Economics, Johns Hopkins University.

James W. Mack, father-in-law of George J. Stigler.

Mabel Waller Mack, mother-in-law of George J. Stigler.

Ruth P. Mack, research staff, National Bureau of Economic Research.

Jacob Marschak, Professor of Economics, University of Chicago.

Edward S. Mason, Professor of Economics, Harvard University.

Joseph L. McConnell, Professor of Economics, University of Illinois.

Lloyd A. Metzler, Professor of Economics, University of Chicago.

Max F. Millikan, Professor of Economics, Yale University.

Frederick C. Mills, Professor of Economics, Columbia University and research staff, National Bureau of Economic Research.

Lloyd W. Mints, Professor of Economics, University of Chicago.

Wesley C. Mitchell, Professor of Economics, Columbia University and Director of Research, National Bureau of Economic Research.

Geoffrey H. Moore, Economist, National Bureau of Economic Research.

Edwin G. Nourse, Chairman, Council of Economic Advisers.

C. Reinhold Noyes, member, Board of Directors, National Bureau of Economic Research.

G. Warren Nutter, Professor of Economics, University of Virginia and research staff, National Bureau of Economic Research.

Leonard E. Read, President, Foundation for Economic Education.

Lionel C. Robbins, Professor of Economics, London School of Economics.

D. H. Robertson, Professor of Economics, Cambridge University.

Wilhelm Roepke, Economist, Institute of International Studies, Geneva.

Paul A. Samuelson, Professor of Economics, Massachusetts Institute of Technology.

Jane Kretschmer Savage, wife of L. J. Savage.

Leonard Jimmie Savage, Professor of Mathematical Statistics, New York University, then Institute of Radiobiology and Biophysics, University of Chicago.

Esther Werth Schultz, wife of Theodore W. Schultz.

Theodore W. Schultz, Professor of Economics and Department Chair, University of Chicago.

Joseph Schumpeter, Professor of Economics, Harvard University.

Carl S. Shoup, Professor of Economics, Columbia University.

Henry C. Simons, Professor of Economics, University of Chicago.

Eugen Slutsky, Professor, Mathematical Institute, University of Moscow.

Vladimir I. Smirnov, Professor of Mathematics, University of Leningrad.

Arthur Smithies, Economist, US Bureau of the Budget, later Harvard University.

David Stigler, son of Margaret and George J. Stigler.

Joseph Stigler, son of Margaret and George J. Stigler.

Margaret "Chick" Mack Stigler, wife of George J. Stigler.

Stephen Stigler, son of Margaret and George J. Stigler.

Leo Szilard, Professor of Biophysics, University of Chicago.

Lorie Tarshis, Professor of Economics, Stanford University.

Ralph W. Tyler, Director, Center for Advanced Study in the Behavioral Sciences, Palo Alto, CA.

John Van Sickle, Professor of Economics, Wabash College.

William Vickery, Professor of Economics, Columbia University.

Jacob Viner, Professor of Economics, Princeton University.

Abraham Wald, Professor of Mathematical Statistics, Columbia University.

Donald H. Wallace, Professor of Economics, Princeton University.

Anne Armstrong Wallis, wife of W. Allen Wallis.

W. Allen Wallis, Professor, then Dean, Graduate School of Business, University of Chicago.

Thomas J. Watson, Jr., Vice President and Board of Directors, IBM Corporation.

V. Orval Watts, Editorial Director, Foundation for Economic Education.

Clair Wilcox, Professor of Economics, Swarthmore College.

Joseph H. Willits, Director, Division of Social Science, Rockefeller Foundation.

Herman O. A. Wold, Director, Institute of Statistics, University of Uppsala.

Leo Wolman, Professor of Economics, Columbia University.

Leland B. Yeager, Professor of Economics, University of Maryland.

Owen D. Young, American lawyer and businessman.

Philip Young, Dean, School of Business, Columbia University.

Introduction

And in any case, only a crackpot would spend seven months staring at the
ceiling and then suddenly begin to read a book by the now ex-officemate
when he knew in advance that he wanted to argue about it.

(George Stigler to Milton Friedman, August 19, 1946)

How in the world do you ever find time to write so many things, all good?

(Milton Friedman to George Stigler, April 7, 1948)

Milton Friedman and George J. Stigler are generally regarded as the pillars
of the modern Chicago School of Economics.[1] To friend and foe of
Chicago economics alike theirs are the names on the Chicago School
marquee. For instance in his article "On the 'Chicago School of Economics'," just three years after Stigler joined the Chicago faculty, H. Laurence Miller, Jr. identified Stigler along with Friedman as the Chicago
School's leadership.[2] Stigler himself questioned the usefulness of Chicago
School as the term was used by Miller and others.[3] Stigler deflected attention from himself, suggesting that when people use the term Chicago
School, they really mean Milton Friedman.

The two men shared much over the course of their lives. They were
graduate students together at the University of Chicago; they were colleagues at the Statistical Research Group (SRG) during World War II, at
the University of Minnesota for a year after the war, and at the National
Bureau of Economic Research through much of their careers. From 1958
until Friedman's retirement in 1976 they were together on the faculty of
the University of Chicago. Both received Nobel Prizes, Friedman in 1976
and Stigler in 1982. And for almost a half century the two personified University of Chicago economics.

This volume comprises the existing correspondence between Milton
Friedman and George Stigler from 1945, the date of their earliest existing

letter, through 1957, the last year the two were at different academic institutions. Their correspondence displays the warp and woof of their professional and personal relationships over a decade that was formative for
them personally, and for American economics. Like so many others,
World War II disrupted their lives. Before the war Stigler was in a tenured
faculty position in the business school of the University of Minnesota, his
first position after completing his doctoral thesis in 1938. Friedman's pre-
war career was less settled. He worked for several government agencies, at
the National Bureau of Economic Research, and left what was expected to
be a tenured appointment at the University of Wisconsin after one academic year (1940–41). During World War II Stigler worked for the Office of
Price Administration and the Statistical Research Group, and Friedman
worked at the U.S. Treasury and the Statistical Research Group. After the
war they made new beginnings of family and professional life. Although
Friedman and Stigler first met in 1934, when Friedman returned to the
University of Chicago from Columbia, they traveled different paths until
working together in New York for the ten months that Stigler was at the
Statistical Research Group. The letters begin very near to the start of their
close friendship.

Friedman began graduate studies at the University of Chicago in 1932.
After a year's work he left for Columbia University, but remained there
for only the 1933–34 academic year. He returned to Chicago in the
autumn of 1934, planning to complete his Chicago doctorate. Stigler
arrived at the University of Chicago in 1933, having begun his graduate
study in economics at the University of Washington. They first met in the
autumn of 1934 when Friedman came back to Chicago from Columbia.
They were together at Chicago for the 1934–35 academic year, then went
their separate ways. There is little evidence to suggest that Friedman and
Stigler were especially close before their reunion in 1944 in New York,
where they served on the staff of the Statistical Research Group.[4]

In the first letter of this collection, Friedman wrote on May 19, 1945, to
respond to a report from Stigler of his efforts to secure an appointment for
Friedman in the Business School of the University of Minnesota. As the
war moved toward its end the Statistical Research Group was disbanded,
and Stigler returned to his faculty position at Minnesota from which he
had been on leave. Two weeks after VE Day (May 8, 1945) Friedman was
among the SRG staff still in New York winding up the group's work. His
letter reveals that prospects appeared poor for a Minnesota appointment.
Ultimately Friedman received an offer from Minnesota, just prior to the
start of the autumn 1945 term.

Although they had known each other for a decade, it appears that Friedman and Stigler only became fast friends while they were at the SRG over

ten months in 1944–45 and then as they shared an office at the University of Minnesota through the 1945–46 academic year. There are, not surprisingly, no letters from the year Friedman and Stigler were officemates at Minnesota. The correspondence picks up after they parted in the summer of 1946. Both had resigned from the University of Minnesota, Stigler to take a position in the economics department at Brown University and Friedman to join the economics faculty of the University of Chicago.

The year at Minnesota marked not only the deepening of Friedman and Stigler's friendship but the beginning, and superficially the end, of their professional collaboration. They wrote a critique of rent controls, *Roofs or Ceilings?*[5] Conflict with their publisher, the Foundation for Economic Education, over the content of the article filled the letters of the summer of 1946. *Roofs or Ceilings?* was to be the only piece of which they were coauthors. Yet the letters show that there was a great deal of collaboration on research, albeit without both their names on the author's line. The letters show each man imprinted his mark on the other's scholarship. This is especially so of their work on price theory. Although they have been referred to as the "Mr. Micro" (Stigler) and "Mr. Macro" (Friedman, for his work in monetary economics) of Chicago economics,[6] both contributed substantially to Chicago price theory. Their contributions include both Stigler's and Friedman's price theory textbooks;[7] Stigler's work on monopolistic competition, basing point pricing, the Giffen paradox, the history of utility theory, and economies of scale; and Friedman's work on the Marshallian demand curve and methodology. The letters show them struggling to reach agreement on how to read Alfred Marshall's *Principles of Economics* and on the significance of this half-century old book[8] for modern economic analysis. Marshallian price theory was to become a key component of Chicago School doctrine, but in 1946 it was far from clear that this would be the case.

After their departure from the University of Minnesota until 1957 Stigler and Friedman were at different universities, Stigler at Brown University for one year and thereafter at Columbia University, and Friedman at the University of Chicago. They were reunited in 1957–58, when they both had fellowships at the Center for Advanced Study in Behavioral Sciences in Palo Alto, CA. Then in 1958 Stigler joined the Chicago faculty as Charles R. Walgreen Distinguished Service Professor of American Institutions in the Graduate School of Business and Department of Economics. The letters in this volume are restricted to the years 1946 through 1957 when Stigler and Friedman were at different universities. There are letters from the years they were both on the Chicago faculty in the Milton Friedman Papers at the Hoover Institution and the George J. Stigler Papers at the University of Chicago, but the correspondence from the early period is of more historical interest. These letters are from the formative periods in their careers and give a fuller picture of their personal and professional relationships than letters from 1958 on. This was also a crucial time for the University of Chicago department of economics, which had an almost complete turnover of faculty after the war. The Friedman–Stigler letters from this period are also set against the background of an emerging post-war consensus among economists covering ideas of what constituted good economic theory and of the value of economics to society. This was a consensus that George Stigler and Milton Friedman ultimately helped shape, but nonetheless from which they were estranged.

The correspondence provides a bridge between the memoirs of George Stigler, *Memoirs of an Unregulated Economist* (1988), and those of Milton and Rose Friedman, *Two Lucky People* (1998). Stigler's book contains less information about the details of his life than the Friedmans' book. He wrote a mostly intellectual autobiography, using his life experiences as a starting point for commentary on economics and economists. The Friedmans' memoirs are mostly about their personal lives together, with less intellectual biography, and relatively little in the way of commentary on economics and other economists. The Friedman–Stigler letters provide us with personal biographical detail missing from Stigler's memoirs and commentary on economics missing from the Friedmans'. They also give a unique, behind-the-scenes look at two giants of twentieth century economics.

Among the topics of the early letters is the unsettled state of Stigler's and Friedman's academic careers. After World War II there was considerable movement of economists between universities. In the spring of 1945 as Stigler lobbied his colleagues at the University of Minnesota to make an offer to Friedman he reported that there was little progress. Friedman replied with suggestions based on his work with the Statistical Research Group that Stigler might use to win over those opposed to his appointment. When he arrived at the University of Minnesota Friedman moved into a shared office with Stigler, and they soon began collaborating on *Roofs or Ceilings? The Current Housing Problem.*[9]

While they were together at Minnesota the University of Chicago Economics Department voted to hire Stigler to replace Jacob Viner, who had departed for Princeton. But after Stigler's interview with President Ernest C. Colwell the university administration vetoed his appointment. Subsequently the position went to Friedman. Stigler accepted a position at Brown University, and he and Friedman left Minnesota at the end of the 1945–46 academic year. Stigler suggested to Friedman soon after his arrival that Brown was a pleasant place, but there were not any really good students or faculty there (gs to mf, November 1946). Columbia University had a vacant economic theory position, and arrangements were made for Stigler to commute to New York to teach theory on a temporary basis.

Stigler then emerged along with A. G. Hart as a candidate for the position at Columbia on a permanent basis.[10] Arthur F. Burns was one of Stigler's primary supporters on the Columbia faculty. Friedman wrote in November 1946 that he had seen Burns, who was not hopeful for Stigler's chances (mf to gs, November 27, 1946). The gossip at Chicago, where they were also recruiting A. G. Hart, was that Hart had been selected for the Columbia position. Stigler replied that prior to a recruiting luncheon with the Columbia faculty Burns warned him to, "remember they are ministers." He continued, "needless to say, at most I wasn't a devil" (gs to mf, November 1946). Hart got the Columbia position but Arthur Burns was successful in persuading the department to request a second position. Columbia's central administration granted this and it was offered to Stigler.

Stigler's judgment of the quality of faculty at Columbia was little better than his assessment of his colleagues at Brown. He reported that he found William Vickery to be a "colorless mathematician," whose "students are in almost open revolt." He found Hart to be "neither wonderful nor horrible," and concluded that "by comparison I guess I'm wonderful – I have over 100 [students], with 2 standing up this week" (gs to mf, November 1946). In 1948 Stigler told Friedman that "Columbia is now looking for a European Institute economist, and for a Far Eastern Institute economist – would that we were allowed to look for a good economist" (gs to mf, October 1948).

Meanwhile in Chicago Friedman was lobbying his department to recruit Stigler. He reported in November 1946 that there was no change in the level of interest for Stigler, but there was one discouraging development. The faculty had voted for an offer to Paul Samuelson. Friedman wrote:

> We don't yet know the end of the story. But whatever it is, I am very much afraid that it means we're lost. The Keynesians have the votes & mean to use them. Knight[11] is bitter & says he will withdraw from active participation in the dep't. Mints,[12] Gregg[13] & I are very low about it. Brown [University] or [Johns] Hopkins may be pretty good after all.
>
> (mf to gs, November 27, 1946)

One can easily suppose today that when Milton Friedman joined the University of Chicago faculty in 1946 this was his dream job, returning to his sentimental alma mater to replace his teacher, Jacob Viner.[14] But the letters reveal that during his first couple of years at Chicago he was uncertain that he was settled. The summer before Stigler moved from Brown to Columbia he expressed disappointment with Columbia's delay in an effort to recruit Friedman. Friedman told him that Burns's presence in New York was the only thing that would make Columbia attractive to him. If Stigler was also there, this would "therefore double (on grds of economics) & more than double (on grounds of bridge) the attraction" (mf to gs, December 2, 1946). In 1947 and 1948 Fritz Machlup pressed Friedman to consider Johns Hopkins. With the potential of a higher salary plus better location for his work with the National Bureau of Economic Research, Friedman asked Stigler, "Tell me, from the fullness of your experience, together with my indifference curves, how large a price ought I to pay for the privilege of being at Chicago?" (mf to gs, April 7, 1948).

Efforts by the two to get themselves together at the same university continued through the 1950s, with Friedman and his colleagues at the University of Chicago twice making overtures to Stigler. Financial and family considerations, along with the proximity of the NBER, kept Stigler in New York, but he commented in 1951: "It seems fundamentally improper for us to be at different schools and I don't like to continue the impropriety" (gs to mf, June 1951). After trying unsuccessfully to land Arthur Burns for Chicago upon his resignation as Chairman of President Eisenhower's Council of Economic Advisers in 1956, Friedman remarked: "Having failed on Stigler & Burns, & being a believer in judging hypotheses by their conformity to experience, I am not sure I can accept your characterizations of Chicago & Columbia. The proof of the pudding seems to be in the beating we have gotten" (mf to gs, December 5, 1956).

In the fall of 1956 Friedman and Stigler both accepted invitations to spend 1957–58 at the Center for Advanced Study in the Behavioral Sciences, in Palo Alto, California, "Ford Heaven" as Friedman referred to the Center.[15] While they were in Palo Alto the University of Chicago Graduate School of Business finally succeeded in drawing Stigler away from Columbia.[16] So when he and Friedman left the Center, they did so as colleagues, their desire at last fulfilled.

In the summer of 1946 Friedman wrote to Stigler that he was reading Alfred Marshall's *Principles of Economics*[17] along with Stigler's *The Theory of Price*[18] in preparation for his first class at Chicago, in the autumn quarter. The questions he raised began a series of exchanges on Marshallian and Stiglerian price theory. This topic occupied a substantial portion of their correspondence for several years (at least until 1951) and contributed to ideas for research and teaching for both Stigler and Friedman. A comment of Stigler's in the summer of 1946 sums up the tone of their exchanges on Marshall: "I do not wish to attack Marshall; although your overpraise certainly invites it.... It wouldn't be fair, but I'd bet money that students reading only my book would get better grades on your exams than those reading only M[arshall]" (gs to mf, September 1946).

A price theory issue that occupied their interest early in the correspondence concerned the chapter in Stigler's textbook on demand theory and the properties of indifference curves. Friedman disputed Stigler's assertion that "the principle of an increasing S_{yx} [marginal rate of substitution] corresponds to the older theory of diminishing marginal utility of a commodity as its quantity increases" (Stigler, 1946, p. 71). He tried with a mathematical proof to convince Stigler that the argument was wrong, and the ensuing discussion occupied them through several letters. Another exchange in August 1946 concerned Friedman's comparison of Marshall's and Stigler's methods of proving the Law of Diminishing Returns, and how one distinguishes between a priori and empirical proofs. Friedman wrote:

> And this noontime I was comparing what Marshall and Stigler had to say on the law of diminishing returns. Stigler, pp. 116–25; Marshall, Bk IV, ch. III, par. 1, pp. 150–3 in my edition.[19] Marshall is very convincing; Stigler says, in effect, that Marshall is guilty of "question-begging" [p. 119], that his "and similar proofs are essentially tautological" [p. 120]; yet Marshall sounds anything but tautological, he sounds realistic and as if he were basing his results on sound observation. As nearly as I can figure it out, Stigler has a sound point; but with little trouble Marshall can be rehabilitated, and, when he is, is far more convincing than Stigler.
>
> (mf to gs, August 12, 1946)

In the autumn of 1946 Stigler was investigating the historical evidence for the Giffen paradox. He mentioned this project to Friedman and promised to send a paper, concluding, "meanwhile it is clear (1) Marshall doesn't shine, (2) the evidence for the paradox is deeply hidden" (gs to mf, November 1946). Shortly afterwards Friedman sent comments on Stigler's "Notes on Giffen Paradox" (mf to gs, November 27, 1946). He liked the paper and suggested that Stigler send it to the *Journal of Political Economy*, which "is desperate for material and would be overjoyed at getting your note. It may be too good for the JPE – but why not bring the JPE up instead of the other way."[20]

Price theory assignments and exam questions were also of mutual interest to Friedman and Stigler, and in several letters they traded potential questions and answers. Some of these were included as problems in later editions of Stigler's *The Theory of Price* and in Friedman's *Price Theory: A Provisional Text*.[21] In November 1946 Friedman wrote to Stigler:

> I am going to start picketing you long distance. "Stigler is unfair to teachers of economic theory." I wanted to assign some standard problems – dumping & price leadership & index no. – & lo & behold, they are all worked out in Stigler. I am enclosing a couple of problems which I finally worked out to get around Stigler's unfair competition.
>
> (mf to gs, November 27, 1946)

The three-year period of 1946 through 1948 was a crucial time for the development of both the content and methodology of Chicago price theory. Stigler's *The Theory of Price* came out in 1946. This textbook was an augmented version of his *The Theory of Competitive Price*.[22] The book's size was doubled. There were new sections on "The Theory of Imperfect Competition" and "Multiple Products and Capital and Interest" along with the earlier book's introductory material and treatment of "The Theory of Competition." In June 1947 Edward Chamberlin published a review of *The Theory of Price*,[23] and this became the catalyst for Stigler's critique of monopolistic competition in his London School of Economics lectures.[24] Six years earlier, in 1941, Friedman wrote his first published piece on economic methodology, a brief review of Robert Triffin's *Monopolistic Competition and General Equilibrium Theory*.[25] In late 1947 he began working on "The Methodology of Positive Economics," and in the spring of 1948 he began "The Marshallian Demand Curve."[26] The latter was both an interpretation of Marshall's theory of demand and a critique of Walrasian economic methodology. So the theory and the methodology of monopolistic competition were provocation for Stigler's and Friedman's elaborations of Chicago price theory and methodology.

Stigler wrote to Friedman in August 1947 for advice on if and how he should make a public response to Chamberlin's review. He had replied privately to Chamberlin, accepting some points of criticism, but objecting to the overall thrust of Chamberlin's criticism. His letter to Chamberlin says:

> And I am distressed that my failure to accept the theory of monopolistic competition is a crime, per se. This may be so, but it requires proof. I criticize your distinction between production and selling costs; you are silent. I disagree with your abandonment of the industry concept and explain why; you are silent. I argue that combinations are of basic importance; you find this irrelevant as if my task is to do justice to theories instead of reality. . . .
>
> In any event, it is not a sin to reject your orientation; in this I have very illustrious companions. I am prepared to argue (1) that your theory is indeterminate and (2) that it is not useful (often) in realistic

analysis. I do not recall a single consistent application of it to a real problem, and this is the ultimate failure of a theory.

(Stigler to E. Chamberlin, August, 1947)

After seeking Friedman's advice on whether to write a reply for publication Stigler chose not to reply directly in the *American Economic Review*. Instead he began a paper that became one of his five London School of Economics lectures, "Monopolistic Competition in Retrospect." Upon reading a draft of the lecture in November 1947, Friedman told Stigler that he thought the piece was on the right track, but that it did not go far enough. Friedman sent a copy of his review of Triffin's *Monopolistic Competition and General Equilibrium Theory*, and wrote,

> I have gotten involved for various irrelevant reasons in a number of discussions of scientific methodology related to the kind of thing you are talking about. In the course of these I have been led to go farther than I had before in distinguishing between description and analysis and in discarding comparisons between assumptions in reality as a test of the validity of a hypothesis.
>
> (mf to gs, November 19, 1947)

He made the argument that in practice there is an inverse relationship between realism of assumptions and success of hypotheses that rationalize masses of facts, suggesting that his own idea was similar to that which Stigler was developing for the lecture.

In the summer of 1948 Friedman sent Stigler an early draft of his methodology essay, then titled "Descriptive Validity vs. Analytical Relevance in Economic Theory." Stigler said that he would like to see it published, but that he thought Friedman would face criticism for not pursuing the question of how one can judge before hypotheses are tested which assumptions are most promising. He gave as an example of what he meant a problem on which he was working, the theory of basing point pricing:[27]

> If I predict basing points in industries where the geographical pattern of consumption is unstable, you (I hope) will find this worth looking into. If I predict basing points in industries where Yale men are over Princeton men, and love to rib Fetter's disciples, you sneer, although you haven't a shred of evidence that the latter is inferior in predictive value to the former. It is surely possible to say something about some assumptions being more promising than others, and yet not to take back any of the things you are saying at present.
>
> (gs to mf, September, 1948)

Friedman's defense of his position led to discussion of different stages in the development and testing of scientific hypotheses. He replied:

> I'm inclined to argue that the logical counterpart of the intuitive process whereby we reach such judgments is a process of indirect testing, that our so-called theories are not separate, concrete, disparate things, but fit together into some kind of a whole. And what is involved is that we have certain phases of our theory in which we have a good deal of confidence because they have stood the test of experience, that certain kinds of assumptions or kinds of theories have in those fields turned out better than others, and that that's the real basis for our confidence in one theory or another. Thus, to take your example, we would be unlikely to have much confidence in predictions made that basing points will arise in industries where Yale men are over Princeton men simply because that kind of a theory, that kind of a set of assumptions, isn't one with which we've had very good luck in the past. We don't have any tested segment of economic theory which uses that kind of data. On the other hand, we might be interested in a theory that basing points will arise when the geographical pattern of consumption is unstable, because that does tie in with some other elements of our theory that seems to yield correct results. This is all very hazy and sketchy but it seems to me to suggest the direction in which one wants to go.
>
> (mf to gs, October 4, 1948)

In his 1949 article "The Marshallian Demand Curve" Friedman makes claims on two levels. These are that, (1) on the history of theory level, economists commonly misinterpreted the content of the *ceteris paribus* condition in Marshall's demand curve, and (2) on the methodology level, the conventional interpretation was less useful for analysis of real-world problems than his own interpretation. The conditions ordinarily held unchanged along the demand curve included money income and the prices of every other good. Friedman argued that Marshall meant for the *ceteris paribus* conditions to include real income and the prices of closely related products. Under the conventional interpretation a change in the price of the product whose demand is represented by the curve would cause a change in real income. Under Friedman's interpretation, the price change would be accompanied by an opposite change in prices of goods not closely related or a change in money income, in either case to preserve the level of real income.

Friedman sent Stigler the first draft of the essay in June 1948. There followed a flurry of letters over the next five months, of which seven remain. Six are letters from Stigler to Friedman, which suggests that there are four or five missing letters from Friedman. Stigler received the paper while packing and doing last minute chores before leaving New York for Canada for the summer. His immediate reaction was that Friedman was misinterpreting Marshall.

> You take the positions (1) he was realistic, and (2) he was a magnificent logician, and seek for an internally and externally consistent interpretation of what he says. In this I think you are too generous. If your interpretation is correct, you have convicted him of complete illiteracy; not even in his mathematical appendix does he give explicit support to you.
>
> (gs to mf, June 21, 1948)

Five days later, while still in the midst of preparing for the trip to Canada, Stigler sent another reaction after checking Marshall's first edition, which he had suggested that Friedman also consult. On this basis he judged Friedman's interpretation "wrong, though splendid." His advice at this point was to "put it on ice for quite a period and then rewrite it," because the argument was presented so defensively and subtly that it would not convince the general reader (gs to mf, June 26, 1948). On the tenth of July, after having the leisure to study the paper in Canada, Stigler professed to be "carried away with admiration for the industry and analytical skill the Marshall paper displays, but am not ready to accept it" (gs to mf, July 10, 1948).

Friedman must have rebutted the suggestion that he "ice" the paper, for Stigler wrote on July 26 that he agreed that this was a good time to write, "[having] all the dope at your finger tips" (gs to mf, July 26, 1948). He still insisted that it was not good to publish "in the flush of discovery and controversy." He predicted that by December one of them would convince the other. The first response from Friedman that we have is dated October 4. He denied two of Stigler's interpretations of "his" demand curve, that he was excluding the Hicksian income effect altogether and that individual demand curves could not be aggregated.

> I am merely arguing that he [Marshall] held the purchasing power of money in the market sense constant. . . . On this interpretation I don't see any difficulty at all in adding the demand curves of individuals. The question is, what would be the quantity purchased by Mr. A or Mr. B or Mr. C if the price of sugar were such and such, and the price index number such and such. That's a straightforward objective question, and I don't see why it raises any difficulty in adding demand curves of different individuals.
>
> (mf to gs, October 4, 1948)

In the final letter on the Marshallian demand curve, Stigler stuck to his argument that Friedman is reducing to zero or trivial the income effect of price changes.

Friedman made two extended visits to Europe during the five-year period from 1950 to 1954. From September through December 1950 he served with the Marshall Plan agency, the Economic Cooperation Administration (ECA), in Paris. He returned to Europe in August 1953 to spend the academic year on a Fulbright Fellowship at Cambridge University.

Two of Friedman's letters to Stigler remain from when he was in Paris with the ECA. They give his impressions of economic conditions in Europe, the Germans and Germany after the war, the Cold War threat from the Soviet Union, and the life of a bureaucrat in an international agency. He wrote the first letter three weeks after arriving in Paris, reporting that the family was living in a magnificent house with a maid and use of a car. He felt that he and the other Americans were treated much too well, with a real income roughly double what they had at home (mf to gs, November 15, 1950). Upon his return to Chicago in January 1951, Friedman told Stigler that the only disappointment in his experience in Europe was that he had to put in too many hours in the office, accomplishing too little. "I can't say I did anything worth while. I wrote a bunch of memoranda to be neglected; saw a lot of people; found out quite a lot about Europe; found out how much I didn't and still don't know and how much a handicap it is not to be fluent in the language of the country you stay in" (mf to gs, January 15, 1951).

Friedman's impressions of the European economies were that they were highly rigid and monopolized, and that by comparison the American economy was perfectly competitive. He found that even visiting American steel and aluminum industrialists whom he encountered in Europe were shocked by the anti-competitive practices there. The European conception of free enterprise was "freedom for everybody to protect his particular vested interest of the moment" (mf to gs, January 15, 1951). He also found in Europe a high degree of income inequality, which he thought, along with monopoly practices, was exacerbated by direct controls over international trade. Previewing his famous article on flexible exchange rates (which had its origins in one of the ECA "memoranda to be neglected"), Friedman told Stigler that he thought an absolute precondition for liberalizing trade was that the Europeans move to flexible exchange rates.[28] "If you or I were in charge of one of those economies and had to operate with rigid exchange rates under present day conditions I very much fear we would use direct controls over trade too" (mf to gs, January 15, 1951).

Soon after their arrival in Europe the Friedmans took a weeklong automobile trip to Germany. The experience was traumatic, as Friedman recalled to Stigler:

I have seldom had so strong an emotional reaction as I did when we first drove into Germany. All the hatreds of the years suddenly spilled out in a tremendous revulsion; every face I saw was a Nazi face – & people since have told me that maybe I was right ... we both [felt] so strongly that the first day we drove until 4 o'clock in the p.m. before eating lunch so we could get to an American Army snack bar. This feeling got much moderated as we saw & talked with Germans & found them, of course, pleasant normal human beings.

(mf to gs, November 15, 1950)

In addition to the hatreds and destruction of World War II, Friedman was concerned about the threat of the next war, with the Soviet Union. He found that, apart from the British, Europeans were resigned to being occupied by the Russians. Few continental Europeans favored a strong defensive commitment. Arriving back home, he found only a little less defeatism. "Before leaving Europe I was inclined to say that there was one chance in four the Russians would attack in the Spring; I'm now inclined to double the chances after seeing the degree of disunity and defeatism here" (mf to gs, January 15, 1951).

Four years later Friedman sent Stigler a letter giving an account of four weeks of travel in Spain, Sweden, and Denmark during his sabbatical year at Cambridge University. He found Spain extraordinarily interesting and the Spanish people wonderfully hospitable, and recommended that Stigler put Spain on his list of places to visit during his upcoming (1955) sabbatical. The issue of most interest to Friedman about Spain was what life was like for the Spanish under the Franco regime. He reported that there were no propaganda pictures of Franco displayed except on money, and that casual conversation seemed "utterly free." But in the conversations he had with his Spanish hosts, he was told not to be misled by this freedom of expression, for nothing beyond speech was free (mf to gs, May 25, 1954). Friedman found a full array of periodicals in the university library, including *The Nation* and *The New Statesman* from the political left. He saw social and economic policy that indicated a welfare state, with extensive government ownership and control of industry. He remarked on the inequalities of wealth and income and the extreme poverty of those who were the least well off. He expressed surprise that in a right-wing country the younger Spanish economists were predominantly Keynesians and planners in the British sense.

Of the two Scandinavian countries the Friedmans visited from Cambridge, he found Sweden the more interesting. This was in part because Sweden seemed so much like the United States. The land and man-made structures of the Swedish countryside, the farming practices and industry, all looked and even smelled to him like New Hampshire, where he regularly summered. He attributed the similarities to the industrial revolution coming late and at the same time to Sweden and the United States, and to both countries being spared since then from the physical destruction of war. The Swedish economists he met also impressed him, especially Erik Lundberg (mf to gs, May 25, 1954).

In the winter and spring of 1955 it was Stigler's turn for an extended visit in Europe, spending a half-year sabbatical in Switzerland. Stigler does not appear to have traveled as much as Friedman, and when he did so he was a less thorough reporter of his experiences. The one letter in the collection from Switzerland reports Stigler's impressions of the Swiss economics literature and policy. Stigler had been reading the Swiss literature on cartels, and found it "very sad." He attributed generally bad Swiss policy to bad economic analysis. "I've been reading a fair amount of Swiss economic literature and I am impressed by how much of the error of their ways – or so I see it – is due to very poor economic analysis" (gs to mf, May 14, 1955). One manifestation of this that he cited was resistance to fluctuating exchange rates, which Friedman had begun to advocate while in Paris with the Economic Cooperation Administration.

These are but a few of the topics discussed by Stigler and Friedman in their letters. Stigler sent much of his work to Friedman for comment. There are letters discussing his papers on the development of utility theory, Ricardian economics, and the functions of local government.[29] The letters have some surprising gaps in topics. Only one letter from 1945 to 1958 mentions Friedman's work in monetary economics, and there is relatively little on his work on consumption theory. In addition to economics, the letters contain details about pregnancies, children's illnesses, vacation experiences, house-buying efforts, and other day-to-day experiences that allow one to see Milton Friedman and George Stigler as fathers, husbands, and friends.

Sources of the letters are Milton Friedman's office files and the Milton Friedman Papers in the Archives of the Hoover Institution, the George J. Stigler Papers in Regenstein Library at the University of Chicago, and files in the possession of Professor Stephen M. Stigler of the University of Chicago, Department of Statistics. The combined collections contain over 200 pieces of correspondence, of which 71 are included in this volume. In addition, the volume includes nine letters between Stigler or Friedman and other individuals that are related to the letters between themselves. The letters are arranged chronologically. A word about dates and ordering is called for. A number of the letters that Stigler wrote have no date, and we have used the letters' contents to estimate the dates on which he wrote them. Estimated dates are enclosed in brackets. In some cases the estimates are of an exact date, for example [August 27, 1946], other times a month or season, for example [August 1947]. Where two or more undated letters have the same estimated date, for example December 5 [1949] and [December 1949], we estimate their chronological ordering.

We have silently corrected typographical and other simple errors in the originals, and left in place or noted errors that may have meaning for readers. Abbreviated words are completed with additions in brackets except for cases where the abbreviation will be obvious to readers. We identify the people who Friedman and Stigler mention in the letters in a dramatis personae, except authors of works mentioned who were not living when the letter was written, for example Adam Smith. The identifications are with respect to the time of the letters. Thus, for example, Arthur F. Burns, who later was Chairman of the Federal Reserve Board, is identified as professor of economics at Columbia University, Director of Research at the National Bureau of Economic Research, and Chairman of the Council of Economic Advisers. When Freidman and Stigler refer to a person by given name or nickname only, we provide the full name in the footnotes. Books and articles to which the letters refer are identified in footnotes, as are unpublished or not-yet published work and events that are discussed. We use footnotes to provide facts that illuminate Friedman and Stigler's discourse, but keep interpretation to a minimum so as not to impart bias in how the letters are read. We wish to let the authors of the letters speak for themselves.

The editors wish to thank, first of all, Milton Friedman and Stephen M. Stigler for permission to publish the letters. We have received helpful comments from Ross Emmett, Don Moggridge, George Tavlas, and two referees for Routledge. Our student, Dominic Constandi, transcribed letters and provided research assistance. Our thanks also go to Gloria Valentine, Laura Gammons, Jane Hammond, and Joanne VanSice.

Letters

467 Central Park W.

New York 25, NY

May 19, 1945

Dear George:

Many thanks for your (no) progress report.[1] Sorry though not too surprised at your report of squabbling. The variability about the mean seems remarkably small – one university faculty, even the best, is pretty much like another.

Two points occurred to me that might be useful to you – though probably neither is since both are on the rational rather than political level. Both are perhaps directed at Kozelka[2] more than the others.

1. Sequential analysis has, as you know, been declassified. Both theory & applications will appear in some form or other in the near future.[3] Its main application has been in industry, as you know. I would have rather special competence to teach sequential, &, if I came to Minnesota, Minnesota could be one of the first to reveal the secret weapon to an eager public.

2. As you know, I have been working on a manual on sampling inspection for the Navy.[4] In that connection, I've had a chance to learn a good bit about quality control & acceptance inspection. It has occurred to me that business schools have been missing a golden opportunity. Quality control & the like have been monopolized by engineering schools. Largely as a result, I think, it has been very poorly developed along rather arbitrary and simple lines. It seems clear, however, that it pretty definitely involves economic considerations as well as technical considerations. It's a rather nice economic problem to try to figure out, for example, what kind of an O[perating]C[haracteristic] curve[5] a business firm ought to buy; or what

multiple of σ [standard deviation] they should use in setting control limits. Technical considerations do enter in – statistical & engineering. But they are, like in other economic problems, simply given data. The field could accordingly be developed at least as well in a business school as a branch of business management as in an engineering school. The business school that first takes it up, & gets someone to develop it along economic lines could, I think, make a killing.

I have developed some interest in the problem & would not be averse to giving a quarter course or so in it. At the same time, it is obviously not something I would have any interest in for any long period. Consequently, I should just as soon not be committed to working in the field.

If you think, however, that it is the kind of consideration that might cut some weight, I would have no objection to your using it.

The first point, on sequential, you might well know of your own accord. The second is a bit more ticklish. If you want to attribute it to me, you might say I mentioned it in conversation – or something like that. You will know better than I how to put it, though.

Nothing much new on the New York front. As you know, a possible fight is brewing between [Thornton] Fry & us over sequential applications.[6]

How's the family? Our's is fine.[7]

Many thanks,

Milton

University of Minnesota
School of Business Administration
Minneapolis

June 23, 1946

Dear George:

I am enclosing a note I got from Mints in which I thought you might be interested.[8] Of course, accident or no accident, it doesn't change the terrible fact, but somehow, one would feel a little less bad about the business if it were an accident rather than suicide – though rationally, perhaps the reverse should be true.[9]

You did pretty well on your deal with Read,[10] it seems to me. Nice work. Please let me know how much the phone call you made to me was, or rather, put it on the bill that is accumulating.

The trip out here was uneventful.[11] We had some minor motor trouble – the radiator hose sprang a leak. But otherwise no incident except the difficulty of finding a place to sleep.

This is a wonderful place, except that it is still somewhat too cold here. Rose & the kids are fine. Trust you all are too.

Yours,

Milton

[late July 1946]

Dear Milt:

I've had the thing retyped,[12] doing virtually nothing to your version except put in some sub-headings.

I bought that 6 bedroom affair[13] – I'll send a snapshot, and am going to retire to Indiana until September.[14] Now all I need are stove, refrigerator, telephone and income.

I misplaced your Portland [Oregon] address & therefore did not send it to Watts.[15] You might drop me a card with it.

Regards,

George

August 7, 1946

Mr. V. Orval Watts
The Foundation for Economic Education
Irvington-on-Hudson
New York

Dear Mr. Watts:

I am enclosing the housing paper in a revised version. You will observe that many of your suggestions have been adopted, and both Friedman and I think that you did an excellent job of editing the manuscript.

On the other hand, various suggested changes have also been deleted. We have sought to keep more of the original tone of dispassionate evaluation, whereas your suggestions accentuate its polemical character. We feel that our approach is somewhat more effective and, in any case, is the way we feel and write.

Of the various specific points raised in your letter, the following deserve some comment:

1. On pages 4 and 5 your revision changes the point of the argument. We argue that inequality is bad but is no special reason for rent controls; your version suggests that inequality and its consequence are good.

We do not argue for heavier taxes, but for heavy taxes.

2. The statement you inserted on page 8 argues that rent controls are inflationary. We do not believe that a clear case can be made that controls aggravate inflation. The comparison must be made between credit now used to purchase housing and credit which would be used in a free market to purchase and build housing.

3. The census material you insert is difficult to use. The 1945 data pertain to a period when demobilization was far from complete. The data call for fairly extensive analysis because they seem to suggest both an increase in housing facilities and a spreading out of families. We think that on balance the inclusion of these data would bring more confusion than strength.

4. Your division (page 16) was reversed: $111/31.3 = 3.55$; apparently you divided 31.3 by 111. We still feel that removal of rent ceilings would lead to lesser increases of rents than you state. Friedman, who followed developments in Portland closely, fields strongly on this point, and I concur.

5. I agree that in terms of direct argumentation, the last two paragraphs are somewhat of an anti-climax. But we think they are indis-

pensable in giving the tone of objectivity we seek. We are seeking to convince the open-minded, not those who already favor our position, and we think these paragraphs help do this.

If the present version is acceptable and is sent to the printer, will you please see that galley or page proof is sent to Friedman and me? I shall be back at 231 North 6th Street, Indiana, Penn., if proof is sent out this month.

Sincerely yours,

George J. Stigler

[early August 1946]

Dear Milt:

Read[16] called & asked permission to delete (1) "like us" in the equality discussion on page 5,[17] (2) the last sentence p. 5, beginning "Further, the pers[onal] inc[ome] tax."[18] He also wishes to add subheads, but says they will be descriptive, in our tone. I said that I thought deletion (2) was OK, but would consult you on (1). Also, if you wish either in, telegraph or call (collect) Leonard Read, Found. for Econ. Education, Irvington-on-Hudson.[19] I got a little sore at his insistence on (1), not because it's imp[or]t[ant] or directly relevant to our article, but because he insinuated that they would not publish it with this in. I told him that if you were inclined to desire it in, I would be quite indifferent whether he published it, and that tune seemed to die down.

He will print 10,000 copies as is. Then he'll make a 16 page condensation for the Nat[ional] Real Estate Assoc., for which he has a confirmed order of 500,000. On the condensation, we are to be shown it. I don't know whether we should ignore it or ask for [an additional] $500 – after all, we sold the article as was, not all of this revising job.

I leave for Indiana tomorrow.

Regards

Geo[rge]

The Waves
Cannon Beach
Oregon

August 10, 1946

Mr. Leonard E. Read
Foundation for Economic Education
Irvington, N.Y.

Dear Mr. Read:

This will confirm the wire I sent you yesterday reading as follows:

Agree to eliminate sentence beginning quote the personal income tax unquote. Consider it essential to retain phrase quote like us unquote from sentence quote for those like us who would like even more equality unquote.

If this phrase were omitted we would almost certainly be interpreted as opposed to more equality. This seems far more serious than possibility we will be interpreted as favoring tax program we do not favor. Sentence in question does not mention specific techniques for achieving equality and omission of other sentence eliminates any reference anywhere to a specific technique.

I believe it essential to make it clear wherein we are criticizing means and wherein ends. Failure of liberals to emphasize their objectives seems to me one of reasons they are so often labelled reactionaries. END OF WIRE.

After sending this wire, I received a letter from Stigler which suggests that you must have misunderstood him. He too had no object to deleting the sentence "The personal income tax etc" but did have real doubts about deleting the phrase "like us."

Your sentence "Your article capable of wide circulation and usefulness but we consider it essential not to support worse evils while combating rent control" puzzles me. Do you intend to imply that publication by you is contingent on our willingness to delete the phrases you object to? I sincerely hope that this is not your intention. But on the off chance that it is, it would perhaps be well for me to indicate my position, with which I am sure Stigler agrees. I should like to see the article published in the form in which it was written or with the revisions to which we agree. If it cannot be published unless we delete phrases we wish in and you do not, then I should prefer it to remain unpublished.

I should add that we are very grateful for the careful criticism Mr. Watts gave to the article. Most of his revisions were excellent and much improved the article. As you know we accepted most of them.

In view of the extent of revision of the article, I consider it essential that we see the final page proof before the article is published. You know where to reach Stigler. I can be reached at The Waves, Cannon Beach, Oregon until Aug. 18, at 335 S.W. Woods Street, Portland, Oregon until Aug. 29, and at Department of Economics, University of Chicago thereafter.

Sincerely yours,

Milton Friedman

August 12, 1946

Dear George:

I got the carbon of the revised rent article[20] this morning and can find only one typographical error in it (p. 3, line 5 under I, where*ver* should be when*ever*). I think I independently sent you my Portland address: 335 S.W. Woods St.

But the main reason for this letter is a very different phase of the problem of rent: the law of diminishing returns. As you know, I have been reading Stigler[21] to prepare for teaching; I have been also reading Marshall.[22] And this noontime I was comparing what Marshall and Stigler had to say on the law of diminishing returns. Stigler, pp. 116–25; Marshall, Bk IV, ch. III, par. 1, pp. 150–3 in my edition.[23] Marshall is very convincing; Stigler says, in effect, that Marshall is guilty of "question-begging" [p. 119], that his "and similar proofs are essentially tautological" [p. 120]; yet Marshall sounds anything but tautological, he sounds realistic and as if he were basing his results on sound observation. As nearly as I can figure it out, Stigler has a sound point; but with little trouble Marshall can be rehabilitated, and, when he is, is far more convincing than Stigler. I thought you might be interested in a brief discussion of the point, and it gives me an excuse to get it down on paper (I am making a carbon of this letter for my files).

Says Marshall (p. 150) "We learn from history and by observation that every agriculturist in every age and clime desires to have the use of a good deal of land; and that when he cannot get it freely, he will pay for it, if he has the means. If he thought that he would get as good results by applying all his capital and labour to a very small piece, he would not pay for any but a very small piece." To restate: If the law of diminishing returns were not valid; i.e., if the application of additional units of labor and capital to a piece of land yielded constant or increasing returns, then individuals would have no incentive to get additional land and we should observe in fact that individuals used and wanted very little. Our hypothesis leads us to expect a certain result, we find that result, hence our hypothesis is not contradicted.

True so far as it goes, says Stigler, but there is a hidden assumption, namely that the whole production function is of a very special class (of which linear homogeneous is the chief example). Stated differently: the hypothesis of diminishing returns to variable proportions is not enough to explain the general desire for land; nor, if properly supplemented, is it the only hypothesis that will explain this fact. Suppose additional[24] labor and capital applied to a piece of land yielded diminishing returns, but increasing labor, capital, and land yielded still more rapidly diminishing returns; then people would still till very small plots and let the rest of the land lie idle. But this hypothesis is contradicted by the facts, so can be rejected. Suppose, now, additional units of capital and labor yielded constant or increasing returns when applied to the same piece of land, but increasing capital, labor, and land yielded more rapidly increasing returns. It would then follow that people would have a great desire for land, as we observe. This is Stigler's sound point. The facts Marshall adduces are consistent with his hypothesis; but, says Stigler, they are also consistent with an alternative hypothesis.

To rehabilitate Marshall, it is only necessary to see what flows from the alternative hypothesis. Does not this alternative hypothesis imply that whoever got started first in adding land, capital, and labor to his initial supply could outbid anyone else just getting started? Hence, if the alternative hypothesis were valid, we should expect to observe not only that men everywhere desire to have the use of a good deal of land but that everywhere a few (perhaps only one) and only a few succeed. Agriculture would be organized in gigantic farms and most farmers would be hired laborers. This we do not observe; hence the alternative hypothesis is contradicted; and the original remains the only simple hypothesis consistent with the observed facts.

Can we go one stage farther and rehabilitate Stigler by taking account of the fixed factor of entrepreneurship? I think not, though I haven't thought this through clearly. The attempted rehabilitation would proceed by setting up another alternative hypothesis consistent with the two facts so far stated. Suppose there is increasing returns to additional labor and capital applied to a fixed amount of land and entrepreneurship, still more rapidly increasing returns to additional labor, capital, and land applied to a fixed amount of entrepreneurship, and still more rapidly increasing returns to an increase in labor, capital, land and entrepreneurship. Then since one individual can provide only a limited amount of entrepreneurship, the two observed facts would follow, together, of course with enormous increasing external economies to the agricultural industry (since I have two entrepreneurs with two units of labor, capital, and land producing more than twice what one entrepreneur with one unit of each produces). But are these for the world industry, or for one nation? If the latter, the nation that started first would presumably eclipse the world. And of course, I am, in effect, denying the validity of experimentation: the same circumstances do not give the same result; but that is on a different level. In any event, I doubt that you will like this rehabilitation, though I should leave that for you to say.

You may ask, why all this fuss when Stigler accepts the law on other grounds, namely, technological experiments. The reason is that <u>economic</u> empirical evidence of the kind given by Marshall is intellectually far more satisfying to an <u>economist</u> than technological evidence. In addition, part of my purpose is to show that Marshall here as elsewhere, was proceeding on a truly scientific basis, not on that tautological, formal basis that enervates so much of modern theory.

And so to close, while you contemplate ecstatically the increasing returns from size of house and estate.

Yours,

[Milton]

[August 19, 1946]

My dear collaborator:

I called up the boys on Saturday morning and found that the damn thing was already in type and they weren't promising that they would be able to change anything.[26] Nevertheless I read my list to them and then mailed them a copy. We shall see.

Let me say at the outset, in commenting on rent, that I resent comparisons with Marshall,[27] who did not even play a good game of auction.

You say that <u>economic</u> empirical evidence is intellectually far more satisfying than technological evidence. I cannot claim even an intuitive understanding of this statement. Diminishing returns is technological, so you prefer an indirect to a direct proof:

1. Because you are freed of dependence on non-economic data? Perhaps, but this is clearly a move in the direction of a closed, formal system – which you don't like.
2. Because it is more efficient? That depends on the case.
3. Because it is more elegant? No, this is pure formalism.
4. Because?

The big trouble with an indirect proof is that by the time it becomes rigorous it is usually terribly complex and cumbersome. Of course you did not even begin to fill the holes in Marshall's argument. How about non-economic institutions, such as inheritance? How do you handle constant returns, which would presumably lead to wide variety of size (which we observe) and yet, with just a touch of entrepreneurial diseconomies, does not get out of hand. How do you know that your demonstration that one nation may monopolize a commodity does not explain a considerable range of facts?

As a matter of fact, I am coming to believe that you are more consistently abstract and a priori-ish than I. But it's cloaked over by your emphasis on realism, which I would like to have you define. I shall conjecture, if only to hasten the enlightenment, that you like a firm skeleton of rigorous theory well skinned with concrete illustrations, in the manner of Marshall and Burns,[28] all oriented in accordance with your general view of how economic life runs. In any case, I do.

As a digression, it is worth remembering that Marshall often, perhaps usually, thought of diminishing returns as an historical law describing the returns to land as population grew. And I doubt that this was in any real sense scientific; it was an idea acquired from earlier economists that casual observation did not refute.

And in any case, only a crackpot would spend 7 months staring at the ceiling and then suddenly begin to read a book by the now ex-officemate when he knew in advance that he wanted to argue about it.[29]

George

Aug. 23, 1946

Dear George:

I am enclosing correspondence from Watts[25] [letter to Friedman, August 19, 1946]. I did <u>not</u> follow his request to return one copy indicating which changes I agree to. It's none of his business. All he needs is what we jointly decide. I shall drop him a note saying that I have sent you my comments [notes with handwritten comments, n.d.] & you will send him the chges we jtly agree to. My comments are on the enclosed copy of his suggestions. Is this ok by you?

We leave [Portland] Tuesday for Chicago & will be there Thursday.

I sold the car yesterday for $1150! Almost $300 more than I paid for it 6 yrs & 33000 miles ago.

I'm rushing because Rose & the kids are waiting for me.

Yours,

Milton

Our best to everybody.

August 19, 1946

Dr. Milton Friedman
The Waves
Cannon Beach, Oregon

Dear Doctor Friedman:

We are sending to the printer your article as it was sent to us by Dr. Stigler on August 7. We shall send you the galleys as soon as they are ready.

At a few points, however, I believe the article was improved by the condensations or deletions.

On a separate page I am listing those which I should like to make in the galleys. You may not approve of any of them. If you do approve any of them will you please mark the enclosed papers accordingly, send one as soon as possible to Dr. Stigler and one to us. Before the article is put into page-proof form, I hope we shall have word from him as to which, if any, of these condensations you both approve.

Very truly yours,

V.O. Watts

P.S. The change in title to "Roofs, not Ceilings," was not my original idea, and it has now become "Roofs or Ceilings?" I hope the change in order of words, at the suggestion of one of the officers of our organization, does not annoy you too much. My own preference was for your title, but I considered the point too unimportant to be worth arguing.

You doubtless know that Dr. Stigler is back in Indiana, Pennsylvania.

Page numbers refer to the manuscript sent us by Dr. Stigler on August 7.

Page 3, last sentence in the third paragraph under the heading, I. The 1906 Method: Price Rationing. "Similarly, if the demand for any article decreases, the price tends to fall, expanding consumption to supply and discouraging output."

This fills out the "economic theory" of equilibrium price, but probably clutters up the argument and distracts attention, as far as the lay reader is concerned. I would delete it. [Holographic marginal note from Friedman: "G.J.S. Leave in? I don't much care."]

Page 13, first paragraph under, III. The Method of Public Rationing, now reads "The defects in our present method of rationing by landlords are obvious and weighty. They are to be expected under private, personal rationing, which is, of course, why OPA [Office of Price Administration] assumed the task of rationing meats, fats, canned goods, and sugar during the war instead of letting grocers ration them. Should OPA undertake the task of rationing housing facilities? Those who advocate this course argue that the rationing of housing facilities by a public agency would eliminate the discrimination against new arrivals, against families with children, and in favor of families with well-placed friends." [Holographic marginal note from Friedman "On the whole prefer as is."]

I would delete the first 3 sentences, and begin the paragraph, "Those who advocate the rationing of housing facilities by a public agency argue that this would eliminate the discrimination. . ." This change would get into the argument more quickly. It may also avoid the distraction of appearing to raise irrelevant, controversial side issues – namely OPA rationing of commodities. Even if price controls are reestablished on foods after August 20, I do not believe the majority of people would prefer rationing to the "private, personal rationing" which went on from the war's end to July 1 this year.

On the same page, at the foot, and for similar reasons, I would eliminate "One may arbitrarily assign a certain number and type of room to each size or kind of family, but experience with gasoline and fuel oil rationing should warn us that the problem is not so simple." Most people would have to make an effort to recall the problems of gas rationing, and it will appear to many readers to be raising a controversial side issue. [Holographic marginal note from Friedman: "I am pretty indifferent. On whole lean to deleting this sentence."]

On page 14, at the end of the first full paragraph, I would delete, "Obviously, the immense variety of personal circumstances would make the rationing of housing the most complex – and probably the most capricious set of decisions ever made by OPA." Again, this seems to call for an evaluation of OPA in its many aspects, something that is not strictly relevant for your article. You have made your point by illustrations, that is, by your questions, and at the foot of the same page you have another general condemnation of public rationing which serves the same purpose as the sentence I would omit. [Holographic marginal note from Friedman: "Ditto. Indiff. perhaps better to omit."]

Page 17, the long paragraph explaining how subsidies for new construction will cause a depression will throw most readers into a tailspin. It is long and involved. Dr. Stigler suggests for the condensed Real Estate edition a condensation of this and the preceding paragraph as follows:

> "The use of a subsidy in the midst of our high money incomes and urgent demand for housing would be an unnecessary paradox. The successful use of subsidies would after some years allow rent ceilings to be removed without a rise in rents. But building costs would still be high so housing construction would slump to low levels and remain there for a long period. Gradually the supply of housing would fall sufficiently and the population rise sufficiently to raise rents to remunerative levels. Subsidies thus promise a depression of unprecedented severity in residential construction and it would be irresponsible optimism to hope for a prosperous economy when this great industry was sick."

Since saving space is not a consideration in this Foundation version, that paragraph could be expanded or broken in two, if you wish. But at any rate I believe the original should be simplified and condensed.

I would also explain the meaning of "successful" as applied to subsidies. You really mean, "If the subsidies stimulated building and resulted in an increase of housing to the point that rent ceilings could be removed without a rise in rents..."

Perhaps the paragraph could read something like this:

> "The use of a building subsidy in the midst of our high money incomes and urgent demand for housing would be an unnecessary paradox. Now, if ever, people can afford to pay for the housing they use."
>
> "However, [deleted and replaced with "For the more distant future," by Friedman] if subsidies did stimulate building and increase the supply of housing so that rent ceilings could be removed without a rise in rents, the result would be disastrous. Building costs would be maintained at levels which make impossible an adequate return on an investment in housing at current rentals. In fact, the effect of the subsidy would be to raise these costs still further. The present disparity between high building costs and low rents would be frozen into the economy, resulting in a long-continued depression of unprecedented severity and length in residential construction. And it is irresponsible

optimism to hope for a..." [Holographic marginal note from Friedman: "He has a point, but I don't like [this suggested paragraph.] I like [your paragraph above] better; and in the few minutes I have now, I can't fix anything else up. Can you handle this?"]

On page 20, middle of the second paragraph, I would delete "Rationing by public authority could in principle be directed toward helping this group; but it would do so – very cumbrously – only by compelling others to use less housing space than they wish at present rents."

You have disposed of government rationing so thoroughly in preceding sections, that I do not believe you need mention it again as a possibility. Furthermore, it seems to me that your phrase, "in principle," is open to question. Probably you mean, "it would be hoped by its proponents," or words to that effect. If it is good "principle," or "theory," it is good practice. If it is bad practice, I believe there is something wrong with the principle. It is a "weasel" phrase, in my opinion, which lets the reader wiggle out of the logic of your argument. In short, I believe that sentence considerably weakens your argument and concedes more to government rationing than your earlier sections on the subject. [Holographic marginal note from Friedman: "Ok. Fix up next sentence to read: Rationing by higher rents would aid this group by inducing many others to use less housing and would therefore have..."]

Finally, I would omit the last sentence of the article, namely,

"The reason why current opinion is so strongly in favor of the continuation of rent ceilings is that these other evils are less direct, more distant, and, most of all, less obviously the consequence of government intervention."

This is a weak ending, or, perhaps I should say it weakens an ending which is already somewhat apologetic. It is an involved sentence and idea. And as an explanation for rent ceilings, it seems like an excuse or a justification. If the evils are "less direct, more distant, and ... less obviously the consequence of government intervention," some people will conclude that they are not worth bothering about. You have shown that the evils are direct and immediate.

This final sentence really implies that rent ceilings are popular because most people are so short-sighted, lacking in penetration, and gullible. Yet, in its present form, it seems to put the responsibility on externals, impersonal conditions which are too difficult, i.e., "less direct, more distant, less obvious" for people to cope with. Thus, again, it permits the reader to wiggle out of the argument. [Holographic marginal note from Friedman: "There is a good deal in this. Ok by me to omit last sentence."]

Tuesday, [August 27, 1946]

Dear Milt:

Welcome to Chicago, and your beautiful new home. Let me know how it turned out.

Watts[30] called me up this afternoon to say that 5,000 copies of the condensed version had been printed, preliminary to the astronomical printing.[31] Some real estate men saw it and categorically refused to go through with the deal unless we deleted the entire paragraph on the desirability and methods of reducing inequality of income, not just the "like us."[32] The Foundation[33] apparently will go along with this stand.

I must confess that I got sore as hell. I told him that it was intolerable to be pushed about by those punks in the national real estate association, that there was nothing but a little dubious fame in the printing for us and the complete loss of our reputations if we started suppressing our own views (I must have sounded mad because he didn't offer $500 at this point), and that the Foundation itself was in one hell of a position if it was printing only stereotype.

He replied (1) that after all, the income tax is a crime, threatening savings and hence employment, (2) it's collectivistic to have more equality, and we have too much now, and (3) we could always write for equality – in some other place. He sounded as if he had been handed a dirty job and really didn't have any hopes of success. I have not been able to decide why Read,[34] the high-powered funds-raiser, didn't work on me.

I told Watts I would write to you, which you will observe I am doing. If this isn't a bluff, and I think the odds are against it, I am in favor of standing pat and letting the Foundation forget the article and its $650. Moreover, I would then try to get a release from them (remember my contract offer was a fee for the right to publish) and probably peddle it to one or two more places like the SAT ev post[35] before tucking it away in the files. What do you think of these three steps?

If the realtors and the Foundation are representative of the leading defenders of private enterprise, I can draw no optimism from this event.

Last night we set a small slam contract by seven tricks. A good thing too; I've been playing golf for lack of a tennis opponent and I need something to restore my self-esteem.

Your admiring, unpublished collaborator

George

I am reviewing Pigou's *Lapses from Full Employment*[36] – it's unbelievably bad.

Wednesday:

I just got a telegram from Watts. The Foundation is going ahead with our version, and he hopes (but does not promise) that something can be done with the realtors.

[September 3, 1946]

Dear Milt:

These bastards are ever vacillating! You will note [by reviewing the enclosed letters] that I am trying to get the article back free.[37] Should that fail, I am inclined to believe that a full price refund would be the only way to get it, if then. Assuming this is true, I am opposed unless you think we can get it from someone else; after all let's be economic men.

I don't know when I'm going to Brown [University]. Chick's[38] dad is back in Boston (with Mrs. Mack[39]) being checked some more, although he now feels much better. Hence I hate to leave her alone, especially when she's so big we suspect 2, 3 or 4 this time.[40] I have been asked to come and settle the house and I'm going to try to swing it here; I'll know a good deal more tomorrow. I bought from Asa Knowles,[41] that new president of the temporary NY state colleges, as I may have told you. I bought my house at [the University of] Minn[esota] from a man leaving to become a dean; now a president – you do the mathematical induction.

We are all fine – David[42] is very proud of being 3 years old and Steve[43] has lost 2 teeth. I hope your paradise gets fixed up quick so Rose can settle down to bridge, economics, and children, in the order named.

Regards,

George

August 28, 1946

Dr. George J. Stigler
231 North Sixth Street
Indiana, Pennsylvania

Dear Doctor Stigler:

This letter is intended, neither to persuade you to make any further changes nor to apologize, but to try to explain our problems and policies.

First of all, let me say that the position of those who have objected to your declaration in favor of increased equality, I believe, is as much predicated on principle and idealism as your own. I realize that good motives – whether theirs, yours or mine – do not in themselves assure right conduct. On the other hand, it is a mistake to assume that those who disagree with us are necessarily animated by unworthy or selfish motives.

Secondly, we printed and distributed the advance copies of your pamphlet with the paragraph in question because we believed – as you did – that your statement was sufficiently qualified and general that it did not in itself commit you or us to advocacy of any form of collectivism. It now turns out that we (Mr. Read and I) were wrong.

True, a careful reading which notes the significance of everything you say, as well as what you do not say, may not lead to a collectivist interpretation. Frankly, I believe the passage is equally open to several interpretations, even with the most careful study. Whether that is so or not, the fact is that certain thoroughly honest, decent citizens – who favor more forms of equalitarian policy than I do – have interpreted this passage as an endorsement by the Foundation of certain collectivist ideas which are repugnant to us. These same persons also believe that for them to distribute your article would make them share the responsibility.

The effectiveness of words in conveying an author's meaning does not depend on what he, himself, understands his words to mean. It depends on what they mean to the reader. Some of your readers have decided that the words of your article imply endorsement by the sponsors, as well as the authors, of certain ideas which neither they nor we wish to endorse, perhaps ideas which even you do not wish to endorse. Somehow those of us responsible for the Foundation's reputation want to obviate, as far as possible, such an inference or implication. Yet we may be attempting the impossible – a consistent and thorough presentation of the case against restrictionism and collectivism.

When I joined this Foundation, it was with considerable misgivings. In my observation and experience, every organization financed by professed philanthropy (voluntary or coerced) sooner or later becomes a force for demoralizing individuals and thereby destroying liberty. Perhaps the demoralization in the case of our own Foundation is already evidenced in acceptance by Mr. Read and me of a passage which we ourselves considered dubious. We may have been over-anxious to get out a product which we considered "very good, on the whole and in 99 percent of its details." However that may be, when we entered into this organization it was with the intent of never compromising with what we considered to be error. We had seen one organization after another, professing to believe in "free enterprise," or individual liberty, lending itself to promoting restrictions on enterprise and liberty, for the sake of some "greater good" – the N.A.M.[44] with its advocacy of tariffs, chambers of commerce with their demands for local public works financed at the expense of producers in other areas, trade association with their "fair trade" laws and restrictive licensing measures, and so on. We intended – and still do intend – to be one organization which shall at all times present the case for individual liberty and individual responsibility, without concession or compromise and regardless of who may be our opponents. We have fought some of the wealthiest and most influential businessmen and politicians in the past and are ready to do it again at any time and in any way we believe we can be most effective in combating restrictionism and collectivism.

You may think of us as opportunists, interested only in large circulation of our publications and the contributions which may result therefrom, even at the expense of honesty and truth.

I hope that judgment is not correct and never becomes so. Certainly, I have more than once given my employers on other jobs the alternative of letting me speak my mind or dismissing me. In two cases we agreed to part company and in another case I refused to take a job paying double the salary I was getting at the time, because I believed it would involve censorship of my writing and speaking.

Furthermore, Leonard Read is ready now to sacrifice what we have already invested in your piece, amounting to several thousand dollars, rather than put out something that may be interpreted as endorsement of what we believe to be an error.

On the other hand, every intelligent person is in a sense an opportunist. That is, he does not waste his efforts in trying to fight all possible adversaries on every possible point at the same moment. I have sometimes proposed "log-rolling for liberty," instead of for pork-barrel privileges. I am willing to postpone an argument on the protective tariff if I can get the help of a protectionist in fighting some other evil which seems to be a more pressing issue at the moment, such as price control is just now.

Certain educators and educational organizations content themselves with sponsoring "both sides." They rationalize this as a virtue. In my opinion, it is an evasion of responsibility on someone's part and results in degeneration of the persons and organizations in question, as well as injury to other persons. College presidents often use the phrase "academic freedom" to justify retention of professors whose ideas these presidents say they abominate. Out of this has grown the idea that the right of free speech includes the right to be employed and subsidized at the expense of those who may hold quite different ideas.

In this way, most institutions of higher learning cultivate the idea that the truth is promoted by presenting error along with truth. "Taking sides" is frowned upon as "narrow," "partisan," or "propagandist." A teacher gets along with less friction in class or among faculty associates if he is "broadminded," "well-balanced," and "scholarly." The result too often is the stultification of academic minds and a pussy-footing class-room attitude which bring scholarship into contempt and provide fertile soil for utopianism and collectivism.

The question as to whether government should or should not take (further) steps to reduce economic inequality, I should like to have a chance to talk over with you at leisure and at length. My own opinion is that government should concern itself not with equality, but with justice, that is, with securing every producer in the enjoyment and use (including gift or exchange) of what he produces (as measured in free – competitive – markets.)

This means assuring equal "opportunity," insofar as opportunity consists in absence of coercion. I do not believe that government should expropriate the fruits of producers for the sake of non-producers, or of the more productive for the less productive. This Robin Hood policy, however, has now been carried so far that it has stopped the forward progress of American civilization and initiated a decline at a dangerous rate of acceleration. As evidence, consider the intense envy, covetousness, and ruthless greed which have been engendered in millions of lower-income individuals by current equalitarian policies and preachments. These vices always existed, but their political force has now apparently become irresistible in this nation, as well as in others.

It is because of this belief, shared by Mr. Read and others of our supporters, that we have been troubled by the disputed paragraph, and not because we desire to curry favor with the rich or the greedy.

You make an excellent point, however, in saying that we shall have trouble publishing anything on any subject if our trustees adopt the same notions of responsibility as Mr. Read and I have done concerning our own. In fact, we have already encountered the difficulty in the suggestion of one of our most liberal trustees that we put an official disclaimer on every publication. This we oppose as an evasion of responsibility. None of us, therefore, is altogether confident of the outcome of our experiment. Yet we still believe it is possible to oppose certain stateist policies without endorsing any. In that case, since our trustees agree with us in opposing many forms of government restriction, we believe they can each support us as long as we confine our activities to opposition to these things. Only if we began endorsing certain forms of restrictionism or collectivism would we be likely to place any trustee in a compromising position.

Furthermore, we differ from most other "non-profit" organizations in one respect. According to our by-laws, the trustees have no authority to decide any policy matter. They can do only one or more of three things:

1) advise with the president;
2) dismiss him by a majority vote;
3) resign.

Consequently, the trustees have given full responsibility and freedom to Mr. Read. He, in turn, gives similar freedom and responsibility to his associates in the organization. He believes, as I do, that such placing of responsibility is necessary for high-quality work, but continued effectiveness of the organization depends, among other things, upon agreement concerning fundamentals. He and I believe that a reason for failure of certain other organizations to operate effectively in promoting the founders' aims arose from evasion and misplacing of responsibilities, as well as from other causes.

In conclusion, I want you to know that I sincerely appreciate your agreeableness in accepting numerous editorial suggestions. I respect also your desire to preserve the integrity of your thought and argument.

I hope that our next efforts at cooperation, direct or indirect, will result in less friction and more accomplishment. You may never again submit to us a manuscript, and for that I shall be sorry. On the other hand, there may be occasions for cooperation in one way or another, and if they should arise, you may be assured of our sincere goodwill.

With best regards,

Yours very truly,

V. O. Watts

September 3, 1946
231 North 6th St.
Indiana, Pa.

Dear Mr. Watts:[45]

I appreciate receiving your letter, and I look forward to that discussion of equality – there is ample disagreement for an interesting conversation.

Your letter implies that the Foundation[46] will not publish any work that contains a single paragraph that differs from some unspecified platform on which the various members of the Foundation have agreed. This is a feasible policy, I think, only if you intend to use commissioned writers within your group; no matter how "sound" you find an outsider, he will differ on some points from your platform. I should also expect that the better the man, the more numerous would be these minor points of disagreement: you could not publish the articles of Hayek[47] or Henry Simons, or, for that matter, of Ricardo[48] or Adam Smith.

I continue to think that "like us" (or "like the present writers") would clearly eliminate any suggestion of sponsorship. It would not, however, meet the Foundation's objection to publishing anything that contained material which was deemed wrong.

I infer that the Foundation has definitely decided not to publish our article. If this is so, we should like to have a statement from you relinquishing the right to publish it in order to settle the matter.

Sincerely yours,

George J. Stigler

[September 1946]

Dear Milt:

The enclosure [September 6, 1946 letter of V. Orval Watts to Stigler] speaks for itself; now how do we go about getting $500?[49]
I misplaced your last letter,[50] but as I recall, you played around with the various terms in

$$d^2y/dx^2 = -(\varphi_y^2\varphi_{xx} - 2\varphi_x\varphi_y\varphi_{xy} + \varphi_x^2\varphi_{yy})/\varphi_y^3) > 0$$

I, on the other hand, meant that if the above inequality is to hold <u>for all prices</u>, we see by factoring that

$$\varphi_{xx}(\varphi_y - \varphi_x(\varphi_{xy}/\varphi_{xx}))^2 + ((\varphi_{xx}\varphi_{yy} - \varphi_{x'y}^2)/\varphi_{xx})(\varphi_x)^2 < 0$$

And hence that

$$|\varphi_{xx}| < 0 \; |\varphi_{yy}| < 0 \; \begin{vmatrix} \varphi_{xx}\varphi_{xy} \\ \varphi_{xy}\varphi_{yy} \end{vmatrix} > 0$$

Thus the so-called stability conditions require that the marginal utilities diminish and more besides, and this is what my note on p. 71 says.[51] Your criticism is similar to mine this spring that the stability conditions are wrong, and why isn't your answer to me then an answer to yours now?

I have just found your letter, and on the other points I have little dissent. On my organization, I wrote with a view of cleaning up technical details in print so I could spend my time in class on economics and that is what I do. But I do much more of this now than formerly and would undoubtedly approach things differently if I were to start anew. But the organization isn't so important (to me); I get into things like rationing already on demand. The reason I put income analysis first is simply to acquaint the dreadfully ignorant students with some general features of our economic system. You will feel this need too.

I do not wish to attack Marshall,[52] although your overpraise certainly invites it. In a cooler moment you wouldn't praise him for using "unless" instead of "if." But I would like to point out that Marshall means much to you only if you know a good deal. I have used him consistently for text or supplementary reading and all young students, good and bad, have one hell of a time getting much out of him. Sentences that strike you (and me) as luminous generalizations seem to them space-filler. It wouldn't be fair, but I'd bet money that students reading only my book would get better grades on your exams than those reading only M[arshall].

Yours for income from
independent prof[essional] practice[53]

George

September 6, 1946

Dr. George J. Stigler
231 North Sixth Street
Indiana, Pennsylvania

Dear Dr. Stigler:

A printed copy of the extended version of "Roofs or Ceilings?" – just off the press today – will probably reach you before this letter, and you will have discovered what we did about the much-disputed paragraph.

At the time I last wrote you we were debating whether to scrap our work up to that point, or to use a disclaimer foreword or a disclaimer footnote.

None of us wanted any of those solutions, but the footnote finally was agreed upon.[54] The wording is mine, and you can no more be held responsible for what the editor says then he can be held for what you say.

However, the footnote does emphasize, first, that "the authors" are speaking for themselves; secondly, that they have not identified themselves with the collectivists; and thirdly, that, as I see it, the argument is hypothetical, relevant for a collectivist even though irrelevant for an individualist.

You and Dr. Friedman may object to the possible implication of the third sentence of the footnote.[55] However, I believe that what the reader infers from that sentence will depend entirely on how he interprets your own statement in the paragraph in question.

Very truly yours,

V. Orval Watts

vow:vs

Would you and Dr. Friedman care to have some copies for your own distribution? If so, please let us know and we shall be glad to send them to you. V.O.W.

[November, 1946]

Dear Milton:

I do not quite understand your housing problem – isn't furniture for sale? Or have you spent your 1947 salary already? But don't underestimate my labor and troubles – for example I tore out the brick step and laid a new one, thus entering the last of the building trades.

I shall tire of the Columbia trip soon.[56] There was a meeting to pick a successor last week, with Arthur[57] conjecturing that he and Angel[l][58] (for me) would be outvoted by Clark,[59] Goodrich,[60] and one other (Haig?)[61] (for Hart).[62] Apparently he argued well, and Goodrich arranged a lunch this Wed for me to meet the econ. dept, which I did (yesterday). Arthur called up before, and gave me a 4 word message: Remember they are ministers. But needless to say, at most I wasn't a devil. I shall get definite information soon. I hope.

Incidentally, my finances are nothing to brag about. I wrote Carson[63] when I resumed work for the N[ational] B[ureau] and nothing happened. It may be his stupidity, but since I look on the salary as a racket I do not feel like raising an issue.

As I wrote Allen,[64] Vickery[65] is a colorless mathematician and his students are in almost open revolt. Hart, I infer, is neither wonderful nor horrible. By comparison I guess I'm wonderful – I have over 100 [students], with 2 standing up this week.

Brown [University] is very pleasant. The only, but big, defect is that there isn't a single really good person on the faculty and not a single really good student.

I am investigating the Giffen paradox, historically, and when I'm done I'll send you a note on it. Meanwhile it is clear (1) Marshall[66] doesn't shine, (2) the evidence for the paradox is deeply hidden.

Lindblom[67] wrote me a note saying he will probably write the AER a note on the blunder in my article, i.e., that a negative income tax at lower incomes would reduce incentives.[68] Poor Yale.

The family is fine – Steve is wildly enthusiastic over school. We're having an incredible fall – the boys go out in short pants & no coat everyday. Chick is due in a month,– a boy they all say.

Moe[69] tells me that Arthur is pretty well snowed under by administration in spite of (1) half-time at Columbia, & (2) Geoff Moore[70] taking over some work. Incidentally Leo[71] says Johns Hopkins is going to come back with the fancy professorship, big pay & no work.

I haven't seen or received any reactions on housing, except in conversation. Hart thinks it's highly inflationary because landlords will spend the increment, that tenants otherwise would be saving! I'll send you a note I did for some students, who simply wouldn't believe the arithmetic of the price system.

Wald[72] has a book on sequential in preparation, Wiley Publishers say.[73]

Regards,

George

Cisco[74] says there is only one graduate course at Minnesota – [Frederic B.] Garver's.

Nov. 27 [1946]

Dear George:

Your notes on Giffen Paradox are very nice indeed.[75] I have to admit that Marshall[76] does not come out so well. I have almost no comments on your piece. It's very well written & real interesting. My only questions have to do with the statistical parts. Granted that a correlation of $+.213$ or of $+.182$ is not significantly different from zero, & hence does not contradict the hypothesis of a d.c. [demand curve] of zero elasticity (or a range of d.c.'s with neg. elasticity), it clearly contradicts even less the hypothesis of positively sloping d.c. That is, the statistical data on pp 5–6, seem to me rather "to increase our confidence in the validity of the paradox" than "to fail" to do so. In order for the statistical evidence to contradict the Giffen hypothesis, the correlation would have to be negative & significantly different from zero; in order for it to contradict the negatively sloping d.c. – & hence to confirm the Giffen paradox – the correlation would have to be positive & sign[ificantly] diff[erent] from zero. Neither is true. The correlation is pos[itive] but not sign. diff. from zero. Hence the evidence contradicts neither pos. nor neg[ative] sloping d.c. However, the correlation obtained would be observed more frequently if Giffen were right than if he were wrong. To put it differently, the 95% confidence limits on $r_{12.3}$ are $-.26$ to $+.55$ approximately; the correlations within these limits are not contradicted by the evidence on a 95% level.

Your discussion gives the impression that the statistical data are inconsistent with Giffen; though all you can say is that the data are consistent with it – & give it somewhat more support than the opposite – but unfortunately (or fortunately) are inconclusive.

Your Table 1 on p. 8 also seems to me inconclusive. Was the income obtained the income for a single week, as the expenditures were? If so, may it not be that <u>consumption</u> of bread & flour was higher for the lower than for the higher incomes, the excess over purchases being supplied out of stocks? For the 4 lower income classes, both expenditures & quantity vary so little that it would take only a small effect of this nature to reverse the slope. On the whole, therefore, your statistical data seem to me rather neutral & if anything to support Marshall a tiny bit vs Stigler. After all, Marshall did not & would not have argued that the phenomenon was overwhelmingly dominant.

The JPE [Journal of Political Economy] is desperate for material & would be overjoyed at getting your note. It (the note) may be too good for the JPE – but why not bring the JPE up instead of the other way.[77]

We have never settled the dispute about your footnote on p. 71.[78] I can't seem to locate your last letter with the mathematical argument, so let me tackle it by giving an example that disproves your statement.

Take the utility function you used in your pretty numerical analysis of food & housing:

$U = \log x + \log y$.
U = Total utility
x = housing units
y = food units

The indifference curves are given by the above equations with U held constant.

$$S_{yx} = -dy/dx = y/x$$

& S_{yx} obviously increases as y increases relative to x.[79] Also marginal utilities of y & x are decreasing.

Now let us use the utility function

$$U' = e^{2u} = x^2 y^2$$

The indifference curves are of course identical since $x^2 y^2$ is constant when xy is & so is log xy. S_{yx} therefore again equals y/x & is increasing. But

marg[inal] ut[ility] of $x = 2xy^2$ & increases with x
marg[inal] ut[ility] of $y = 2x^2 y$ & increases with y,

& this contradicts your footnote. Q.E.D.

My impression is that the error in your mathematical demonstration was that it left φ_{xy} out of account. But enough said.

I am going to start picketing you long distance. "Stigler is unfair to teachers of economic theory." I wanted to assign some standard problems – dumping & price leadership & index no. – & lo & behold, they are all worked out in Stigler. I am enclosing a couple of problems which I finally worked out to get around Stigler's unfair competition.[80] They are the same problems in somewhat disguised form. The first is a direct steal from Ed Shaw's article on inventories.[81]

I've been waiting impatiently to find out about (a) the additional Stigler,[82] (b) Columbia. I saw Arthur[83] 10 days ago in N.Y. & from his story Columbia does not look at all hopeful. The gossip here, which has not been confirmed, is that Hart[84] was tapped, though we don't know yet whether he is going to choose Co[lumbia] or Ch[icago].[85] Arthur still was hopeful of getting several apptments worked out.[86] I certainly hope from your pt of view that something comes through there, though I have mixed personal feelings. If Col[umbia] gets you I'm afraid we [at Chicago] won't & I just can't tell you how much it would mean to me especially – & some of the rest of us as well – to have you here. I should add that there is nothing new here on your case except for the indirect – & bad – implications of other action. The Samuelson[87] matter was again forced to a head – by Douglas[88] – & thanks mainly to his efforts we lost badly. The dep't has voted to make Samuelson an offer. We don't yet know the end of the story.[89] But whatever it is, I am very much afraid that it means we're lost. The Keynesians have the votes & mean to use them. Knight[90] is bitter & says he will withdraw from active participation in the dep't. Mints,[91] Gregg,[92] & I are very low about it.

Brown [University] or [Johns] Hopkins [University] may be pretty good after all.

We're still living in an empty house & working on it all the time.

I doubt very much that I shall go to Atlantic City.[93] You know about 4E.[94] Whence comes the $.

Here's to the coming depression. (5¢ there isn't one in the next 6 months – not even a picayune recession).[95]

Yours,

Milton

December 2, 1946

Dear George:

You clearly do lead a most interesting life.

I'm delighted to hear about the turn at Columbia. Arthur[96] told me that his tactics were to work for two app'tments & it looks as if he may have succeeded. I would, of course, have been even more delighted had you gotten the first offer as you so clearly should have. But I had gathered that that was extremely unlikely & was afraid nothing at all would come through. So this seems much better than I had hoped. I suppose there is no knowing whether the additional professorship will go through. Here's hoping.

Arthur's presence at N.Y. is now the only thing that would make Col[umbia] at all attractive; your presence would therefore double (on grds [grounds] of economics) & more than double (on grounds of bridge) the attraction. But, as of the moment, it would take an awful lot to make me willing to go through the rehousing mess. Sunk costs may be sunk – but they do give some idea of what costs would be like under similar circumstances again. In any event, the resistance undoubtedly does not diminish in proportion to the attraction: Mills[97] may like my Lange article[98] (as he wrote me he did) but he doesn't like me close; & I fancy he could find enough support to block it. And, our last year's experience should warn us against compounding uncertain eventualities.

Re p.71 n[ote]; you can't evade so easily. I haven't found your letter yet – though I've looked. But I'm reasonably certain it rested primarily on the sufficient condition for a max:

$$\varphi_{yy}\varphi_x^2 - 2\varphi_{xy}\varphi_x\varphi_y + \varphi_{xx}\varphi_y^2 < 0$$

And, contrary to your letter, my $U = x^2y^2$ does not violate this condition. It obviously cannot, since it gives the same indiff[erence] curves as your $U = \log x + \log y$. Mathematically:

$$\varphi_x = 2xy^2, \; \varphi_y = 2yx^2, \; \varphi_{xy} = 4xy, \; \varphi_{yy} = 2x^2, \; \varphi_{xx} = 2y^2$$
$$\varphi_{yy}\varphi_x^2 - 2\varphi_{xy}\varphi_x\varphi_y + \varphi_{xx}\varphi_y^2 = -16\,x^4y^4 < 0 \; \underline{\text{Q.E.D.}}$$

Redouble that if you can.

Hope you can appease the Bur. director,[99] as I'm sure you'll be able to.

We have a bet on the sex of your forthcoming child. I hope you can remember it, because I cannot. But I must have bet it would be a boy.[100]

I'm back at Lerner and am trying really to finish him up.[101] In that connection I've been puzzling about the Keynesian wage flexibility argument, & I think I'm beginning to see some light. I've been putting something down in the form of a letter to Lerner[102] to see what his answer is. If I get it done, I'll send you a carbon – as of course I will of the review when, as, & if it is finished.

Also I've become concerned about the allocative effect of a progressive income tax, & am about ready to assert that it has allocative effects of the same order as special excise taxes.[103] This is particularly nasty (1) because we like the income tax; (2) because it brings out a serious blunder in prof. incomes.[104] I should have compared earnings in diff. occupations net of income tax, rather than gross, as I did.

This last shows the point. Consider an equalizing difference in income, e.g., airline pilots get high salaries to compensate for risk & short working life. Prospective entrants need to look at net returns. Result of income tax is therefore higher gross returns to pilots relative to returns in other occupations than in absence of income tax, lower relative net returns, fewer pilots, less air travel. Is there any difference between this kind of allocative effect & effect of special excise on air travel? Doesn't usual argument about neutrality of income tax (except for labor vs leisure, & risky investments) assume that all diff[erences] in earnings are either transitory or monopolistic? And isn't this far from truth?

More power to your anti-lesterine theory. I haven't yet worked up the energy to read Machlup's[105] attempt. I take it Lester[106] is criticizing [your] minimum wage piece.[107]

X = fingers crossed for
(a) Chick[108]
(b) Columbia
(c) all other good things – but (a) and (b) especially.

Yours,

Milton

[December 20, 1946]

Dear Milt:

I enclose <u>my</u> clarification of the utility problem. It is neater than your handwriting, and gives me a carbon; what do you think of it?[109] You'll notice that I do not dissent from anything you say, poor footnote. Incidentally I enclose a couple errata on problems in my book & will see that you get the answer book soon.[110]

Hayek[111] writes

1. Giffen [Paradox] whips him too (and "old Bowley").[112]
2. I will be invited to give 4 lectures there (London School) if they can raise the travelling expense.
3. I will be offered a visiting prof. next year if Rockefeller[113] is generous. This is apparently confidential so shouldn't be kicked around.
4. A junket to Switzerland in April is contemplated, to save liberalism. I assume you & Aaron[114] would go. If this comes off, (1) train Aaron on bridge, and (2) let's find a fourth liberal; and teach him.[115]

We're reasonably set for Christmas except that parts of Steve's[116] bike haven't come. Jerry (Joe)[117] weighs more than 9 pounds – up $1\frac{1}{2}$ pounds from birthweight in 3 weeks. I haven't done much shopping – poor Chick,[118] and she has done less, poor George.

Chicago is deeply indebted to Schultz,[119] I see. I must complain about your news service. Ann[120] tells me the Savages[121] are there – where? Did Samuelson[122] accept? Will Metzler[123] kill Samuelson? I must tune in on the next letter.

A very merry Christmas

to Rose, Janet, David, and Milton

George

1. The budget constraint on maximum satisfaction merely eliminates one independent variable. Your example, $U = x^2y^2$, can be rewritten as

$$U = x^2(R - xp_x)^2/p_y^2,$$

where x is a free variable. Then for a maximum we get

$$\frac{dU}{dx} = \frac{2xR^2 - 6x^2p_xR + 4x^3p_x^2}{p_y^2}$$

and this equals zero for $x = 0$, $x = R/p_x$, and $x = R/2p_x$.

Turning to the sufficiency condition,

$$\frac{d^2U}{dx^2} = 2R^2 - 12xp_xR + 12\,x^2\,p_x^2$$
$$> 0, \text{ if } x = 0$$
$$> 0, \text{ if } x = R/p_x$$
$$< 0, \text{ if } x = R/2p_x$$

Hence the third value gives a maximum and the other two minima.

2. It is clear, then, that your example leads to finite positive quantities with positive prices, goes to hell if one price is zero, and leads to a positive quantity of y and a negative quantity of x if only $p_x < 0$. Since the indifference curves have horizontal and vertical asymptotes only at infinity this is to be expected.

3. There are two reasons, that may reduce to one, why a form

$$adx^2 + bdxdy + cdy^2,$$

must hold only for small values of the differentials. The first reason is that subsequent terms in the Taylor expansion cannot be neglected if larger differentials are permitted. The second, and fundamental reason, is that there may be several sets of solutions to the necessary conditions. Some maxima may be less than others, or indeed less than some minima.

4. Whatever else follows, it is clear that one cannot infer the stability conditions from stable consumer behavior, because the stability conditions are not necessary. $d^2U = 0$ is compatible with a maximum – if $d^n f < 0$ for the first non-vanishing n.

5. In the two variable case, the conditions on

$$U = \varphi(x_1, (R - x_1p_1)/p_2),$$

are

$$U_1 = \varphi_1 - p_1\varphi_2/p_2 = 0,$$
$$U_{11} = \varphi_{11} - p_1\varphi_{12}/p_2 + p_1^2\varphi_{22}/p_2^2 < 0,$$

where x_1 is a free variable.

Now, I think my trouble was that I was identifying U and φ. They are equal enough, but not their derivatives. The true conditions for a maximum are $U_{11} < 0$ or $U_{22} < 0$, and these do not imply $\varphi_{11} < 0$ or $\varphi_{22} < 0$.

In the three commodity case,

$$U = \varphi(x_1, x_2, (R - x_1 p_1 - x_2 p_2)/p_3),$$

the necessary conditions are $U_1 = U_2 = 0$. The sufficient conditions are $U_{11} < 0$, $U_{22} < 0$, and $U_{11}U_{22} - U_{12}^2 > 0$, and these conditions are also necessary if we rule out $d^2U = 0$.

6. The Hicks-Allen stability conditions are identical with respect to the φ function; they do not use the U function. See Allen, p. 511 top. Their only error is to gloss over the possibility that to a second order of approximation, or to a higher order,

$$U(x_1 + h, x_2 + k) - U(x_1, x_2) = 0.$$

They are assuming, in other words, that the utility function is a simple one. The one fault I find in your Lange article is that the appraisal of theoretical judgments is somewhat subjective. Rising marginal revenues are ok, the Giffen paradox is bad. It may help clear up my worry on this point – although obviously I do not expect that you can eliminate the subjective, which is the only basis in this terrain for separating good from bad people – by telling me why this omission of $d^2U = 0$ is good or bad theorizing.

January 27, 1946 [1947]

Dear George:

Apparently, distance cannot keep you from the insidious practice of wasting my time (& correspondingly improving my mind). Thanks to your proposed question for an exam, I have now spent almost two days working on it to get an example disproving it. I now have one & I refuse to give the question to my class until you explain it away (if you can, ah hah).[124]

The question is a neat one, since it seems speciously plausible. To avoid needless controversy, I quote your statement: "Prove that when there are 2 rationing systems, all consumers gain if one is convertible into the other – i.e., if points may be purchased & sold." I have interpreted "all consumers gain" to mean "every consumer gains," which is what I take it you meant. I tried to construct a proof, & failed; & in the process it seemed to me that the statement was wrong, so I constructed (after much labor, which explains the awkward numbers) a counter example. The point of theory in question is that if consumers who, before convertibility is permitted, are richer in pts than in money ("the poor") have common tastes, & "the rich" also have common tastes (but different from the poor), then I think (though I have no rigorous proof) your proposition is correct. But if among the poor there are a few who have the tastes of the rich, they may lose more by having the price of the commodities they prefer move against them than they gain by being able to convert points into money. (addendum: Something is wrong with this last point, since in one example below, the poor fellow with rich tastes gains along with the rich fellow, while the poor fellow with poor tastes loses.)

Now to roll up my sleeves & give you an example. Commodities X & Y; consumers A & B.

Consumer	Utility f[un]c[tio]n (U)	Initial Money Income (I_o)	Initial Point Income (I'_o)
A	xy	400	200
B	xy^3	100	200
C	xy	100	200

I. <u>Pts may not be bought and sold.</u>

We here have 4 variables (money prices, p_x, p_y; point prices, p'_x, p'_y) and only two conditions (am't of x and am't of y), so any two prices can be fixed independently. However, the natural choice of fixing the two pt prices should not be made, if it is desired to continue the practice after pts are made convertible. Because, if it is, and if not all pts are used before conversion is permitted, then after conversion there is no way for all pts to be used & the money price of pts will fall to 0. This is ok, if you want it, & clearly demonstrates my pt, as we shall see, but to have the game really interesting suppose we fix in advance on p_x and p'_x.

Let $p_{x=5}$ $p'_x = 2$, let total amount of $x = \bar{x} = 65$; total amount of $y = \bar{y} = 37.5$

Then it will turn out that equilibrium values of other items are:

$p_y = 5$ $p'_y = 8$

	x	y	U
Consumption by A	50	12.5	625
Consumption by B	5	15	16,875
Consumption by C	10	10	100

(I leave confirmation of this to you – as an exercise).

II. <u>Points may be bought and sold.</u>
   a. Suppose p'_x and p'_y had been fixed & let P = price of points in terms of money. Then only 430 out of the 600 pts can possibly be used, the price of pts falls to 0, only money matters. The demand curves are:

	x	y
A	$400/2p_x$	$400/2p_y$
B	$100/4p_x$	$300/4p_y$
C	$100/2p_x$	$100/2p_y$
Market	$275/p_x$	$325/p_y$

$p_x = 275/65$

$p_y = 325/37.5$

C consumes of x: $(50*65)/275$; of y: $(50*37.5)/325$

$U_C = (50*50*65*37.5)/(225*325) = (2*2*5*37.5)/11 = 750/11 = 68\frac{2}{11}$
< 100

I could put Q.E.D. here. But let's continue.

b. Go back to p_x and p'_y as fixed & add the condition that the point-money market is to be cleared. Then it turns out that the demand curves are as follows:

For A & C: $x = (I_o + PI'_o)/2(p_x + Pp'_x)$
$\quad\quad\quad\quad y = (I_o + PI'_o)/2(p_y + Pp'_y)$
For B: $\quad\quad x = (I_o + PI'_o)/4(P_x + Pp'_x)$
$\quad\quad\quad\quad y = 3(I_o + PI'_o)/4(p_x + Pp'_x)$

Substitute for I_o, I'_o, add up, equate to the available supplies, and we get:

$$p_x + Pp'_x = (275 + 250P)/65 \tag{1}$$

$$p_y + Pp'_y = (325 + 350P)/37.5 \tag{2}$$

These conditions, via the budget equations underlying the demand curves already imply that the total of money & point income equal (in money) to $(600 + P(600))$ is spent; but they do not assure that the total point value of the goods is equal to 600 & the total money value equal to 600. To assure this, we can add either of the following:

$$xp_x + yp_y = 600 \tag{3}$$

$$xp'_x + yp'_y = 600 \tag{4}$$

If (1), (2), & either (3) or (4) is satisfied, then the remaining one is.

Given $p_x = 5$, $p'_x = 2$, we get
From

(1) $P = 5/12$
(3) $p_y = 22/3$
(4) $p'_y = 188/15$

Combined price:

$$P_x = p_x + Pp'_x = 35/6$$

$$P_y = p_y + Pp'_y = 113/9$$

and these values satisfy (2).

If you now compute the consumption of A, B and C from the demand curves you will find:

	Consumption of x	Consumption of y	Utilities	Utilities before conversion was permitted
A	290/7	2175/113	797	625
B	55/7	1237.5/113	<10,648*	16,875
C	110/7	825/113	114	100

* $55/7 < 8$; $1237.5/113 < 11$; $XY^3 < 8(11)^3 = 10,648$

Ergo B loses, Q.E.D

On monopoly problem: With constant costs & constant supply prices, monopoly price is same as when x is competitive. When I asserted that price when firm also produces $x <$ when x produced competitively, I was assuming rising costs for x. Perhaps I shouldn't do this for long-run. What I had in mind is that if long run supply curve of x is rising (when x is produced competitively), say because of external diseconomies (which will be internal when a single firm is producing the entire output), will not the supply curve of x be the marg. cost curve (to the producer of y) before disintegration, but the average cost curve after? Hence will not the producer of y produce less after disintegration than before? I'm none too sure of this, because I haven't really worked it through.

On Switzerland:[125] we haven't succeeded as yet in getting place on the Queen Elizabeth for Mar. 22nd, but we're still working on it & are optimistic of success. Have you gotten reservations from England to Switz.?

On exam questions: patent owners are reported in the literature as sometimes restricting output of licensees as well as charging a fee even though the patent owner himself produces nothing. How do you rationalize?

Is your answer the same as mine?

Your friend Kozelka[126] is here at the moment interviewing people for next year. Interested?

We're all well; hope you are too.

Milton

January 31 [1947]

Dear Milt,

I was looked over at Yale with serious intent but no overtures. I gave a lousy talk on minimum wages (on which, I protested ignorance but was requested to pander to a large labor management contingent). Lindblom[127] likes it, but has just been offered an assoc. prof in labor at Stanford, and is attracted somewhat by a promised free hand. Millikan[128] is very good; Metzler[129] was affable but ordinary. I hear indirectly that Samuelson turned Chicago down. Next week Johns Hopkins.

On monopoly, preliminary skirmishes indicate that it is a good desert island problem.

On rationing, I wish to emphasize three things

1. The exception proves the rule.
2. What you say is alright in theory but doesn't work out in practice.
3. I had in mind, but not on paper, a much weaker (and stronger) statement: that given the rates of conversion between points and goods and money and goods, each party gains (or in a limiting case breaks even) from conversion between money and points.

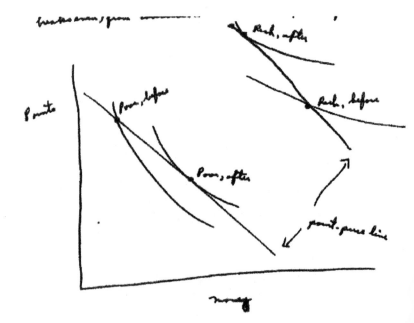

Your generalization raises interesting questions. The real characteristics of point rationing are

1. The points clear the market of rationed goods.
2. Money does not clear the market – for the rich, expenditures $<$ income. Prices are fixed (aside from changes forced by supply factors).
3. Some goods (future included) are unrationed so money does not lose value.

Under these conditions, the unrationed commodity is decisive, and nasty to handle. But if the poor have a point limitation they like the rationed commodities relatively much; if they instead have an income limitation they like the unrationed commodity much. I guess.

In the extreme case of 1 rationed and 1 unrationed commodities, point rationing = specific allotments. Then an answer can be secured. If the poor have income R, the rich nR, x_0 is the allotment, then utility is

Poor $\varphi(x_0, (R - x_0 p_x)/p_y)$
Rich $\varphi(x_0, (nR - x_0 p_x)/p_y)$

assuming identical tastes (a thing no rationer would fail to do). After conversion, if $x_0 = x$ points and p is the dollar price of a point,

Poor $\varphi(x, (R + (x_0 - x)p - x p_x)/p_y)$
Rich $\varphi(x', (nR - (x' - x_0)p - x' p_x)/p_y)$

Then, I hope, to a first term of a Taylor's expansion the new utility of the poor exceeds the former utility by

$$-\delta_x \varphi_{x0} + \delta_x((p + p_x)/p_y)\varphi_{y0}$$

where $\delta_{x = x_0} - x$. This would be zero if $\delta_x \neq 0$ and

$$\varphi_{x0}/(p + p_x) = \varphi_{y0}/p_y$$

But p must be greater than this, or there would be no inducement for the poor to exchange points for money. In fact the symbols are idle: isn't it true that the poor can simply refuse to sell points if they will not gain? (In fact my previous diagram works if money $= y$.) I leave to you the proof for 2 rationed commodities.

And now I must leave the formal playthings of the Chicago school and turn to the hard realism of reading some history of doctrine.

Regards,

George

July 11 [1947]

Dear Milton,

We leave Saturday for Canada, so I'll muse your manuscript[130] for a few days. I've read it once, and while it is perfectly satisfactory, it doesn't pack the Lange[131] wallop; perhaps I may get some ideas.

We're going to visit Arthur[132] tomorrow, for the first & last time. His wife has been very ill, but is considerably better now, which explains our distance. Kuznets[133] is also up here; I ran into him in Hanover. Vermont is beautiful but I still prefer that huge lake in Canada.

Naturally I'm disappointed at Columbia's delay, but I'll continue to hope. With even Yale Brozen getting $7500 (Northwestern) you are the original peon or serf. Cisco[134] says he (Brozen) was personally very objectionable, also that Boddy[135] turned down a good Michigan offer. Cisco, incidentally, is deep in teaching factories inspection procedures, at $2500 per 3 months.

This about exhausts the news, which is scarce on Vermont farms. (Of course you know Homan[136] quit Cornell for Nourse's outfit;[137] shall I get you the editorship of the AER?) The family is fine, and son 3 is handsome, fat, and jolly despite the attentions of his brothers. Tell Rose that 3 is much better than 2.

Regards

George

For the next month:
    c/o James W Mack
    Windermere
    Ontario, Canada

[July, 1947]

Dear Milton

What with 3 sons, 3 nephews, and 2 nieces, 3 brothers in law or sisters in law (with spouses), etc., I'm not optimistic about doing any work the next two weeks. So I send along the Lerner thing with only a few minor comments.[138]

We're having cool to cold weather but hope for a break soon. The boys have a fine time – you should see me paddling a canoe with 5 boys.

Regards,

George

In a fast skimming of the MS, my chief objection is your practice of reciting his failings; it would be much stronger to indicate the type of thing he should take into account.

[August, 1947]

Dear Milt

I'd like your advice on the following matter:

1. Chamberlin sent me a proof of the review of my book in the AER[139] and in reply I sent the enclosed letter.
2. Homan[140] referred to the review (and regretted the fact he hadn't given me opportunity to reply), and I sent a copy of the letter for his own interest.
3. He now writes that I should either quote the central matter or write a short note, for the benefit of readers of our books.

I am not inclined to do this because
(1) of a general feeling against replies to reviews, and
(2) the inappropriateness of a short note in dealing with this matter (and the disinterest in a long one). All I gain by a reply is creation of doubts in the minds of those economists (numerous, alas) who think Chamberlin is a great man. What say?

We're nearing the end of our stay – I have to be in NY Aug. 15 to take over the house. It's been wonderful – a lake (plenty big) 25 feet away, 4 acres of space, a motorboat, etc. I've been busy painting the boat house – white, shutter[141] green, and china red. The boys are brown & healthy as all get out, and my own tan is enviable. But I've hardly cracked a book.

Regards

George

Keep me posted on Johns Hopkins.

[August, 1947]

Dear Chamberlin:

I am not at all angry at your review. It seems to me to make some good points, and in any event it is a sincere expression of an important viewpoint.

In particular, there is a good deal to your objection to breaking up demand, cost, and pricing, and I shall think long and hard when I come to revise these sections.

But I am disappointed that certain charges were made on a misreading, or at least a very unsympathetic reading, of the text, for example:

> Table 18: was designed to show that under imperfect competition the alternative product is the marginal value product in <u>other</u> firms (see last sentence of section, p. 244).
>
> Table 19: I say I am deriving a short run cost curve "for one simple case"; you say that "it is made to appear synonymous and coextensive with imperfect competition."
>
> p. 249: My failure to use monopsony, etc., was deliberate, whether wise or not.
>
> pp. 215, 240: The statements are not inconsistent; for in the latter instance I do not specify complete information.

And I am distressed that my failure to accept the theory of monopolistic competition is a crime, per se. This may be so, but requires proof. I criticize your distinction between production and selling costs; you are silent. I disagree with your abandonment of the industry concept and explain why; you are silent. I argue that combinations are of basic importance; you find this irrelevant as if my task is to do justice to theories instead of to reality. The one point of substantive disagreement is on consumer ignorance, which I hold necessary to monopolistic competition. You concede this only for advertising. But you must either (1) show that there are many cases of many firms producing poor technological substitutes – a class I think is unimportant – or (2) admit my position. Your statement that heterogeneity of resources is sufficient certainly eliminates almost all important forms of imperfect competition.

In any event, it is not a sin to reject your orientation; in this I have very illustrious companions. I am prepared to argue (1) that your theory is indeterminate, and (2) that it is not useful (often) in realistic analysis. I do not recall a single consistent application of it to a real problem, and this is the ultimate failure of a theory. But these are larger issues, which I hope we can thresh out in person.

Cordially yours,

[George J. Stigler]

[October 1947]

Dear Professor:

I have put a few notes on your paper.[142] I dissent from this talk of a consensus of economists. What is true, I think, is that a proposal should be bandied around for a while in professional circles, because logical errors and empirical oversights are likely to be caught. The consensus notion is dubious because the people who fill the journals, – and they're the ones we tend to judge the profession by – (1) are inherently more different-minded, (2) have vested interests in ideas, (3) include some bastards.

I can't make up my mind on publication. The essay is neat and clear and makes some good points. Rather my misgivings are over the desirability of letting yourself in for a lot of work and controversy. But then, you should be willing to be let in for this, if you really want to work this close to policy determination.

Since your proposal is essentially an intellectual skeleton, it cannot make real converts of many people. Sure, publish it.

My own essay is a draft of a lecture, and of course I will welcome incisive criticism provided it isn't too incisive.[143]

I had dinner with Lutz, Gideonse, and Allais.[144] My French is getting worse, and Allais's English no better, so we exchanged no thoughts. Gideonse says Chicago is looking for a polite place to dump Hutchins.[145] And that Watson (IBM)[146] tried hard to get Columbia to take him.

Arthur[147] is busy working Rockefeller for money, chasing to [Harvard] to straighten out a joint research project, and such stuff. I'm going to start a drive for you as Director of Research[148] as soon as I can think of someone to relieve you.

Regards

George

P.S. Get Savage to review Samuelson's new book,[149] or at least the mathematical aspects & appendices.

November 19, 1947

Mr. George Stigler
Department of Economics
Columbia University
New York City

Dear George:

This is just an interim report on the items with which you have been flooding me. We have been in the throes of moving for the last couple of weeks, which explains why I have done absolutely nothing except what I had to and why I have been so slow in responding to you. The worst is over, and I expect to be able to get back to work.

The main point of the interim report is to give you my reaction to your piece on Chamberlin.[150] As you know, of course, I thoroughly agree with you and I think you have done a good job of bringing out the points at issue. I am enclosing a reprint of a review of mine that you might find of some interesting relevance.[151]

The main additional point I would like to make is that you do not really go at all far enough. I have gotten involved for various irrelevant reasons in a number of discussions of scientific methodology related to the kind of thing you are talking about. In the course of these I have been led to go farther than I had before in distinguishing between description and analysis and in discarding comparisons between assumptions in reality as a test of the validity of a hypothesis. I should like to offer the general proposition that every important scientific hypothesis almost inevitably must use assumptions that are descriptively erroneous. It is of the very nature of a really important scientific generalization that it provides a simpler rationalization of a mass of facts than was available before. It is likely to obtain its objective by an inspiration about the particular basic elements of the situation that are important and by discarding what after the event can be shown to have been irrelevant complicating assumptions. In a way, the better the hypothesis the greater the extent to which it simplifies, the more sharply will its assumptions depart from reality.

A somewhat different way of getting at essentially the same point is to ask how one decides what degree of correspondence there is between assumptions and reality. For example, we have the classical equations of physics about how rapidly a body will fall if it falls in a vacuum. We apply these equations to bodies falling in the air by using the hypothesis that they fall as if they were in a vacuum. We want to test the assumption. If we make the test descriptively it is clear that the assumption is much better satisfied thirty to forty thousand feet in the air than on the ground. Yet the theory will apply much better to a body dropped from the roof of a 100-foot building than to the time of fall of a bomb from forty thousand feet to thirty thousand feet. For the second problem a much smaller discrepancy between reality and the assumption is significant than for the latter. The only thing that really matters, therefore, is a conformity between implications and reality, since only after this has been established can one say what discrepancy between reality and assumption is significant.

This is not in any way fundamentally different from the point of view you present, but I think it does give somewhat different emphasis. I shall try in the next few days to send you detailed comment on the Chamberlin lecture[152] and also really to think about your proposed procedure for studying the economies of scale as well as the division of labor problem. The latter strikes me as kind of screwy, but I haven't yet figured out why.

Sincerely yours,

Milton Friedman

MF:IP

[November, 1947]

Dear Milt:

I enclose a letter to Arthur, written with an eye to Willits[153] – what do you think of it? It's all very tentative.

I got your-all blurb, and naturally I enjoyed it. In a first & only casual skimming, I thought the day to day correspondence between prices and M was pressed too hard, but had no other questions. Also I haven't studied your methodology, but it seems so true as to be accepted. But I'll study it – one of the burdens of suburban life is that you leave everything at the office.

I am not prepared to accept your statement that Vickery[154] is ingenious in any important sense. His interests are incredibly narrow. I can make him glow with happiness by arguing optimum prices, but he's bewildered by and indifferent to almost everything else. Re your-all statement, which I retailed at lunch, his great objection was that a rise in interest rates would raise the marginal propensity to consume, so you'd have more inflation. And if you did just a little too much restricting, you'd send us into depression. Besides he pals with Hart,[155] who daily shrinks in stature.

Kuznets[156] is the center of a fight because Shoup[157] doesn't think he's theoretical enough for a historian. Your Colin Clark is very likeable and imaginative, but what are you after – a circus? But who am I to talk of colleagues?

Regards

George

P.S. I hope you realize that Seymour Harris is losing his race with me. I just don't dare send you an article on how smart the classical economists were, or you'll give up completely.

November 24, 1947

Dear Arthur:

In the September 1947 issue of the *American Economic Review*, Hansen states (p. 563):[158]

"...of the $60 billion gross capital formation in business plant and equipment made in the decade 1931–40, 90 percent was replacement investment."

His colleague, Harris, writing in the later-appearing August issue of the *Review of Economic Statistics*, states (p. 152):[159]

"But let us not forget that for the decade of the thirties, gross investment was but $60 billion and net investment was approximately zero."

The comparison suggests at least four comments:

1. The same figure is given for two rather different series; business capital is only part of total capital.
2. The amount of net investment differs.
3. Neither man gives any reference for his figures.
4. The probable source is the Department of Commerce, which has no series with these titles. The most plausible series do not approximate Hansen's $60 billion or his 90 percent.

This almost studied carelessness in the use of facts is very common in economic literature. It is not necessary, or even proper, for me to emphasize to a perfectionist like you the objections to this sort of work. There may be deception. If these errors are widespread and increasing, we may have to give up division of labor. In any event, such errors are more than a symptom of general sloppiness of thought and research procedures, – they are an integral part of that sloppiness. Nor do I need to argue the desirability of improving the quality of economic research and writing.

I believe that real improvements could be obtained by checking a large range of economic literature and publishing the results of the checking. Let me spell out this proposal:

1. The Types of Error
Economists possess their full share of the common ability to invent and commit errors: copying a number wrong, forgetting to tell what number it

is or where they got it, making arithmetical mistakes, relying upon fickle memory, etc. They can reason fallaciously, with or without mathematics. They can misread completely the state of affairs, or reverse the direction of causation. Perhaps their most common error is to believe other economists.

It is impossible to check thoroughly the quality of economic literature, even on a narrow front. Even the most competent economist will be biased in what he checks: he will accept as true the statements or bits of reasoning that he believes and he will examine with critical care the views that are novel or contradictory to those he has been holding. Moreover, there is no ultimate test of validity: even the history of mathematics is studded with universally accepted errors.

Checks of the quality of economic literature should be relatively free of ambiguity as to both (1) what is to be checked, and (2) whether it is correct or erroneous. Two types of material seem capable of fairly large-scale and objective measurement of accuracy:

1. Statements of empirical fact.
2. Quotations from other writers.

Of course one must make concessions to the more or less legitimate desire of an economist to be read. There is no point in checking, or trying to check, (1) sweeping generalizations – capitalism is dying –; (2) widely accepted beliefs – a depression started in 1929 –; (3) the completeness of references to well known sources or series – the cost of living index need not be referred to as compiled by the Bureau of Labor Statistics, referring to clerical and manual workers in 5x large American cities, etc. Nor would I attempt to check paraphrases of the writings of other people, except where specific numbers are involved, since arguable points arise immediately.

The checking of fairly specific statements seems to me eminently useful for two reasons. First, it is not probable that a man who is careless in small matters is careful in large ones; quite the contrary, a man who cannot even copy a sentence of Keynes' correctly is not likely to be a reliable reporter of complicated or badly expressed ideas. Second, it is precisely in these narrower matters that the reader is most at the writer's mercy: a reputable economist, writing in a reputable journal, acquires an aura of reliability, – and after all, we cannot check many things and still do our own work.

2. The Measurement of Errors

I propose that all of the leading American economic journals for some recent year be used as the basis of the tests. This insures variety of authorship and subject, and permits no invidious selection. A group of graduate students could subject each empirical statement and quotation to verification, given suitable training and supervision. I have not explored the problem sufficiently to have very definite ideas on the nature of the tests, but two examples suggest their general nature.

Empirical statements. Hansen, in the article referred to, makes 16 distinct statements of a specific nature about prices and capital formation. Among the relevant tests are:

1. Frequency and accuracy of source. He gives no sources.
2. Adequacy of description. One series – retail food prices – is adequately described; "prices" refers to wholesale prices; "finished goods prices" is a title abandoned 5 to 10 years ago for "manufactured goods prices"; and his capital formation series is ambiguous.
3. Frequency of error. 8 of his 16 statements are wrong. Possibly something could also be done on the magnitude of error. In Hansen's article, for example, 3 of the 8 errors exceeded 5 percent of the correct figure.

Quotations. Bishop wrote an article about Knight's views on utility (in the *Journal of Political Economy*, April 1946).[160] It was probably careful as such articles go, because of its controversial nature, and it was unusually easy to write in a technical sense because all quotations were from 2 works of Knight. Bishop gave 31 quotations, all with references. Of these, 30 were correct references. Of the 30 correct references, 7 departed from the original, in 2 instances drastically.

In articles based on calculations, it would be possible to assess the adequacy of the descriptions, and the accuracy of the results. But a complete verification of a year's work would be a very large task indeed, and perhaps some sampling would be called for.

3. The Benefits of the Study

The benefits of such a study, duly publicized, appear to me to be several and substantial:

1. Economists will be taught a decent caution as readers; we are all too prone to accept unquestioningly the printed word or number.
2. There should be an immediate improvement in the low editorial standards of most of our journals; every editor would edit with more care and demand more adequate references.
3. The tests will remind economists that footnotes are not an occasional token of respect for an obsolete and purposeless tradition. It will come

as a shock to many, I am sure, even to realize that references can be checked.

4. The study may lead to the improvement in the quality of training of graduate students. Most teachers are unaware of the problem of quality, so naturally their students are too. Indeed, the checking of references may become a standard pastime of malicious graduate students – which would be more useful to the students and the profession than the activities of malicious graduate students as I partook in them.

I should be very interested in your opinion of the feasibility and desirability of such a project.

Cordially yours,

George J. Stigler

[December, 1947]

Dear Milt:

I've skimmed your comments on the Chamberlin thing[161] enough to see that they are going to be bothersome, a synonym for useful, and I thank you. It's too late to do anything about the letter, and frankly I still think it shouldn't appear: two items would seem to be piling it on; and the tone of the letter seems a little petulant to me at this distance. And when in doubt, don't print it. Anyway, it isn't important.

I'd like to spend a little space on economies of scale, however.[162] To begin, I have also continuously had your feeling that all is not right, and I can't say I have yet lost it. But first let me take up your points:

1.   If the firm expands from x to 2x, average profits fall from .01x to .0075x; total profits rise from 1.5 to 1. (You seem to view profits like OPA,[163] but this I won't argue.)

 a. Ought the firm to expand? Sure, on these facts.
 b. Is the decision to expand to be interpreted as an increase in size despite private (dis?) economies of scale? Yes, despite diseconomies.

 This industry is making a non-competitive return. Let it be so. Then either (1) small firms enter and produce x, and wreck the big firm, or (2) small firms expand to x and do the same, or (3) nobody but the firms at x can expand, and of course do. But my ratio still traces out economies, and answers the question: will trust-busting raise prices or costs? – and in the negative.

2.   You ask whether economies of scale accrue to stockholders or managers or promoters? They may, of course, accrue to consumers or suppliers of resources also, but this isn't important. If they accrue to firms in the industry, I take it that your problem is that they may show up as costs – excessive salaries, or excessive investment on which interest is reckoned.

 Re salaries: they are not important enough to be of any significance. The SEC[164] gives total remuneration of all officers and directors, 1934–38; it was
 1/10 of 1 percent of receipts, US steel
 7/10 of 1 percent of receipts, Bethlehem
 4/10 of 1 percent of receipts, Republic
 4/10 of 1 percent of receipts, National

Re investment: (1) My "operating costs" is before interest
                    (although not depreciation, which wouldn't
                    change it) and shows no downward slope of
                    cost ratios.
                    (2) Obviously I'd be better off with correct
                    investment figures.

3. Small firms have non-competitive wage rates for tax purposes.
    McConnell (S.C.B.)[165] meets this by calculating the same salary for
    officer-owned corporations as found in a sample of non-officer owner
    corporations. This strikes me as crazy; it would be preferable to calcu-
    late interest this way and attribute the residual to differences in entre-
    preneurial ability – which, however, would be a little
    question-begging on economies of scale. At the moment I'm stumped,
    but say that it is not a problem with firms selling 2–5 millions a year.

4. Your vertical integration commends my ratio. Firm B (which bought
    from A) was a sucker to pay A "profits" as well as a return on invest-
    ment, and by vertical integration it may well become more efficient
    than those firms who are being mulcted by non-competitive suppliers.

I grant that my economies border on profitability. But only in a stationary analysis could this be avoided. A firm is more efficient if it rides a
cycle better, if it introduces new techniques sooner, if it gets its labor
cheaper, if it operates at a steadier output, if it sells at higher prices (at
least for the same goods), etc. Even if I could get a stationary, text-book
long run average cost curve I wouldn't want it for policy purposes. If my
firms differ in product structure, and the big firms also have monopoly
power, then I concede that I underestimate their relative costs – a bias I
can stand if it doesn't produce falling average costs.

On the whole, I admit I was wrong on Colin.[166] He is not the man you
or I would want in that perfect University Arthur[167] wants to found, but he
is personally nice, many of his instincts are on the right side, and he's
much more interesting and provocative, and fundamentally no sloppier,
than Kuznets[168] or some other people in NY or Chicago. And he would be
marvelous in infuriating the Cowles[169] boys, although probably not your
equal.

I suppose you saw the new Dean of our business school is Owen
Young's son.[170] I haven't heard a word yet; his picture was in the *Times*[171]
Saturday, as I recall, and wasn't enamoring.

The meetings remain uncertain.[172] I've ordered tickets, because it turns
out that to continue from Indiana [PA] has a negative cost with Colum-

bia's first class fare policy. But I don't know whether I'll get the tickets. And Steve,[173] who has had a cold, is flirting with pneumonia and is on penicillin.

Regards

George

I've shelved, but not abandoned, the size of the market. This is really an important problem, as I shall try to convince you sometime.[174]

[December 10, 1947]

Dear Milt:

An addendum

You say it is always possible to find a logically consistent theory of events $x_1, x_2, \ldots x_n$. This is true only in the peculiar mathematical sense of being able to concoct an equation with n constants.

1. But a theory has less than n constants, and indeed we have Stigler's Law:

    The gorgeousness of a theory varies with the range of phenomena it embraces and inversely with the number of its constants.
2. The great scientific discoveries have been syntheses of diverse phenomena that previously had defied generalization:

    Newton: joined astronomy, mechanics, optics, hydraulics

    Einstein: joined Newton and curvature of light

    Marshall: joined short and long run theories of price
3. There are plenty of well-established phenomena for which we have no theory:

    The rigidity of monopoly prices[175]

    The basing point system.[176] On this, I find economists (Viner, Smithies[177]) saying it is non or ir-rational – that it does not maximize profits. I think I have gotten on the trail of its logic.

    Is this not also a law:

    If businessmen deliberately adopt and persistently retain a practice, that practice is explicable in terms of maximum profits. (Refer to as Stigler II)
4. Since I am splattering my name about, I'll add

    Stigler's Razor: In dealing with economic theory, always use the most advanced branch of mathematics you can apply.

PS: I got the tickets; Steve seems to be coming along alright. It now looks as if I'll get to Chicago.[178]

[December 15, 1947]

Dear Milt:

Tell Rose[179] to expect another heavy eater for the night of the 29th. Tell her to use plentiful foods; Richard Gilbert forecast on the radio a couple of days ago that there would be food riots by next spring if we don't ration food.

1. On methodology, there's a good deal to say for its essential elusiveness. It seems to me, as it appears to you, that most of the problems are psychological, and that one loses most of the real problems by talking in retrospect rather than in prospect. Ex post it is all neat equations. Ex ante it's a baffling jungle. You don't know even 10 theories that will explain monopoly prices, although in principle there are billions. Stigler II is not a tautology, however: it is a working hypothesis, and can be refuted. Thus, in principle it is possible to find a pure choice between $2 and $1 and watch the individual's behavior. Personally, I'd step in first.

2. On the economies of scale, I shall want to think about your argument, which carries a certain plausibility. But I find it hard to fit into your scheme, (1) the fact that US Steel was formed to extract monopoly profits, (2) your theory emphasizes the heterogeneity of resources, the jig-saw in contrast to the Marshallian view of economic life, and I am not prepared to concede the importance of these phenomena. Suppose I take the position that the urge for monopoly profits outweighs other factors in bringing forth large firms? This may, in fact, would get me into further trouble; anyway I'll think about it.

3. The enclosed is pretty pedestrian but has enough wise cracks to hold your interest, I hope.[180]

4. The other enclosed, the clipping, had a later paragraph that the US is fascistic and reactionary and warmongering, but not in the edition from which I made the clipping. Quite a bit of academic freedom even for Chicago.

5. Confidentially, in the event you do not already know, Arthur has some interest in the NB[181] and Gregg Lewis. In this respect we'd both like your reactions on the *Journal of Business* supplement he just did with Douglas.[182] The text is quite short, in case you haven't read it. I should warn you that the statistical work seems to be quite unreliable. In the 1901 budget study, they fit four types of equations to the data, for example. Type C is

$$x = a + bY + cY^2,$$

with x expenditure on something, Y income. Then one would expect the derivative, marginal expenditure, to be linear in income (Table 1), but very often it isn't. Then in a few cases I checked the tabulated values of Table 1 against the equations, with considerable discrepancies. There are other easily detected internal inconsistencies. I should judge that Gregg did this as a favor for Douglas, since the text is clearly the former's.

We're going to Indiana, Pa, on Dec 21, and on Jan. 1 the family is going to climb on my train en route to N.Y. No doubt a very calm trip, with 3 hellions.

Merry Christmas to all,

George

Saturday, Feb. 7 [1948]

Dear George:

I've just read over for the second time, & thought over for the n'th, your "The Economists & Equality."[183] And I know not what to say. Almost am I convinced. It's a very persuasive paper, with a very intriguing interpretation. Whether it is a correct interpretation of the classical economists, I can't pretend to say. More important, in terms of my own interest, is whether it really offers a way out of the dilemma which you quite properly say I & the other bastard descendants of the classical liberals are in. I don't feel happy, either with my own present or previous position, or with your solution. Yet I can't really say why, in any kind of organized fashion.

Re your solution: "the improvement of the individual" is about as ambiguous a touchstone as "equality." I don't know how to define either. You cite Marshall. In him, "the improvement of man" equals the remaking of other peoples into the image of the Englishman, which is warning enough that this slogan has danger of leading to the narrowest kind of presumptuous provincialism. See, e.g., Marshall, *Principles*, p. 201, for "In this case, Chinese lives would have been substituted for American, & the average quality of the human race would have been lowered." I can't help but feel that you're right in saying Marshall's chief touchstone was what he regarded as improving the human race. But I have always shuddered at Marshall's ethical judgments, at what he thought was improvement. Also, how do noncomparables get compared here? Is lengthening of the average length of life a significant objective? Does the "utility" from it depend only on relative position? How should one balance the "advantage," if any, of lengthening the life span against the disadvantage, e.g., of thereby reducing the variety & richness of men's experience? Don't get me wrong. I don't know the answers. But average length of human life somehow seems to me a thing to maximize – though not at any cost which is where you have me – which depends on aggregate output & is not simply relative. Can this be entirely included in "improvement of the individual?" I doubt very much that it can.

To turn to a number of more specific comments. p. 1, Didn't [John Stuart] Mill end up a socialist? And do you want to distinguish in this way socialism from communism? p. 1, 2nd ¶ [paragraph], line 5 – justice → injustice. p. 8, Don't call this "pseudo-scientific argument" dishonest. It isn't. It's wishful thinking, rationalization, etc., but it isn't dishonest. p. 12, I don't see where emphasis on income redistribution rather than resource distribution is a consequence of emphasis on equality. The argument is that proponents of equality would have done better to have concentrated on distribution of resources.

All in all, I think it is a really good paper &, if you are yourself convinced, I would strongly urge its publication. Your point is neither obvious, widely held, often pointed out, or obviously wrong. It gives to think, which is the chief thing to be done on this level.

I want to think more about the general issue & you may hear from me again.

I hope you are taking over a lot of food. If you have room, buy some for me, bill me for it, & pass it on to our English economists.[184]

Our best,

Milton

Tuesday [April 7, 1948]

Dear George:

I am writing mainly to swell your head – though God knows it must be big enough already. Hayek reports that your lectures were "brilliant" & successful.[185] Indeed, he said yours were by all odds the most successful series of lectures they had ever had. I didn't realize the state of English Economics had sunk so low – though, come to think of it, Hayek was including pre-war experience, so I guess I'll just have to take it to mean that the English are still smart enough to agree with the rest of us.

Jewkes, Harrod, & THE PLAN just arrived.[186] Many thanks.

Your wire was wonderful, but your presence would have been even more so. The conferences were swell.[187] Everybody agreed that the level of discussion was extremely high & that the meetings were quite stimulating. There was enough of a common set of values to prevent irrelevant discussion; yet enough disagreement on means to make the discussion pointed. Ellis[188] was the only real disappointment. He is pretty bad. One nice feature was that Mints[189] showed up very well. He's been so much underrated, that that was really awfully nice. Hayek[190] gave a magnificent public lecture to an overflow crowd; Hardy[191] an excellent lecture to a full house, & Lutz[192] a good lecture to a good house. The students showed wonderful discrimination; the size of the house was perfectly correlated with the quality of the lectures. If you & Arthur had come, the weekend would have been perfect.

Machlup[193] was pressing me to consider Johns Hopkins. As you doubtless know, Smithies[194] turned them down for Harvard. I don't know whether to think about it seriously or not. They would offer 8,000 which with 3,000 to 5,000 from the Bureau[195] makes an enormous differential over the 7,500 plus 4E contract[196] I am scheduled to get next year (7,000 this year). Tell me, from the fullness of your experience, together with my indifference curves, how large a price ought I to pay for the privilege of being at Chicago?

I was interested to hear that Mo[197] is going to Chicago. Allen[198] is still involved in comparing incommensurables & balancing on the fine end of the needle, to get my metaphors thoroughly scrambled.

Your little piece on Tarshis[199] was wonderful. How in the world do you ever find time to write so many things, all good?

The kids don't seem to have missed us while we were away nearly as much as we missed them. They were much more interested in the toys we had brought for them than in our return.

I hope your boys are all recovered from the chicken pox by now & that neither you nor Chick[200] acquired it.

Yours,

Milton

April 8, 1948

Dear George:

Just a note to say that you better pay Arthur[201] off. You will receive the distinguished article award.[202] Please keep this <u>real</u> quiet until you hear officially, or my name will be mud.

Congratulations,

Milton

P.S. Listen to Rd Table[203] April 18. It will be on Canadian Exchange Control, with some Canadians & me, unless plans change.

June 21 [1948]

Dear Milt

I am overwhelmed with last minute chores before leaving for Canada, which we plan to do in a week, so I have given your note[204] less thought than it deserves. Here are a few reactions, however:

1. First, you should read Marshall's earlier editions and other works, not that I expect any harvest.
2. I think you are wrong in attributing to Marshall this meaning of his demand curve. Viz.

You take the positions (1) he was realistic, and (2) he was a magnificent logician, and seek for an internally and externally consistent interpretation of what he says. In this I think you are too generous. If your interpretation is correct, you have convicted him of complete illiteracy; not even in his mathematical appendix does he give explicit support to you.

You cite his statement on purchasing power, p. 95, but what of the one on page 109:

> To begin with, the purchasing power of money is continually chang-
> ing, and rendering necessary a correction for the results obtained on
> our assumption that money retains a uniform value. This difficulty can
> however be overcome fairly well, since we can ascertain with tolera-
> ble accuracy the broader changes in the purchasing power of money.

(Incidentally, p. 97n: ... buyers have not a fixed quantity of purchasing power which they are ready to spend on the specific commodities..." – this, however, refers to specific commodities, and is quoted merely for mischief value.) If the above passage has the nice connotation you give it, I certainly miss it.

Without having worked it out, I think that your interpretation makes Marshall's theory of consumers' surplus erroneous: should he not always subtract out the loss due smaller quantities of other goods, when good A increases; indeed must not, on your interpretation, price changes have no effect on consumers' surplus?

My basic point, however, is that throughout his life, the Walrasian boys screamed at the partial equilibrium view of economic life, as manifested by A. Marshall. Now it is certainly true that a partial equilibrium theory always involves logical inconsistency – its excuse is that the inconsistency is quantitatively negligible in a wide variety of cases, and that in exchange for this inconsistency one can say many useful and correct things about how an economy works. Marshall and his pals (Edgeworth,[205] etc.), it would seem, tacitly took this view; certainly they had ample opportunity to come out and say that their demand curve was an aggregative general equilibrium one and so far as I know, never did. (Incidentally, try to find a basis for your interpretation in the works of his prize students – Pigou, Chapman,[206] etc.)

Side remark: on your paragraph on complementarity, see Mathematical Note VII.

Side remark: Is your remark, p. 13, that on the new interpretation the negative slope of the demand curve must be negative an inductive generalization or a deduction from indifference curves?

Side remark: Since the Giffen paradox was also applied to all England by Marshall, you are straining things a bit.

In sum: if on further reading and reflection you agree with me that Marshall didn't mean this, I still think that this note – which is ingenious and beautifully lucid – should be published, although then as what Marshall should have done. But even here more work is called for: do you really think this is a good type of demand curve? I have a feeling that it will cause many more problems than it solves, e.g., its applicability to the demand curves of entrepreneurs, the index number ambiguity, etc. If on further reading and reflection you disagree with me, I am willing to engage in further reading and reflection myself.

The enclosed note[207] is a little crude, but I want your reaction on it. If by irony one can reduce the number of casual inelasticities, and hold this practice open to ridicule, some good will be done; I am not sure that his would do the job.

Gossip: Galbraith and Smithies[208] are going to Harvard. This must mean Samuelson[209] is whipped – surely they can't go and ask for a third Keynesian; unless there are now so many that they don't have to ask.

Gossip: I turned down $5000 to teach 2 days a week for a semester at Buffalo[210] and am still feeling poor.

If you should meet an economist named Burns, A.F., this summer, try to get him to write a treatise on investment in the cycle. I hope, by the way, for your sake as well as ours, that you will take a leave next year to be with us and [at] Princeton; after all, a $15,000 sinecure and good company are not to be sneezed at.[211]

I am finishing the draft of my teacher study; I'll send you a copy in the fall when I've worked it over a little. I'm also doing a little work for an article on basing-point prices, but on the whole have few commitments. I'm fairly seriously contemplating a large study of oligopoly price, oriented in good part toward the type of cyclical and historical phenomena

Abramovitz emphasized in his QJE article on oligopoly[212] But that lies in the future.[213]

Our address this summer will be c/o James W. Mack, Windermere, Ontario, Canada. I expect to go to Seattle around the middle of July and return to Canada about the first week in August, so I shall be much busier than I would like.

Regards,

George

[June 26, 1948]

Dear Milt:

I've looked at Marshall's first edition[214] and at your MS[215] (=Marshall satirized?) but I haven't had time to do much with either – we're off to Canada in 2 days.

On this preliminary basis I think that your interpretation is wrong, though splendid, on the following grounds:

1. He begins the principles (I, I, 5; first edition throughout, though the 8th is similar throughout):

   > Throughout the earlier stages of our work it will be best to speak of the exchange value of a thing at any place and time as measured by its price, that is, the amount of money for which it will exchange then and there, and to assume that there is no change in the general purchasing power of money.
   > (note). In this we are only following the practice of the ordinary business of life, which invariably starts by considering one change at a time and assuming for a while that "other things are equal." As Cournot[216] points out ... we get the same sort of convenience from assuming the existence of a standard of uniform purchasing power by which to measure value, that astronomers do by ...

   Thus purchasing power (of money, not income) is constant everywhere – not just in demand theory. I assume this means, in the light of other remarks, that an index number such as the B.L.S.'s[217] remains fixed.

2. Hence Marshall doesn't need to repeat this assumption in demand theory, and he <u>doesn't</u>:
   BK III, II, On the law of demand – doesn't list it
   Similarly, pp. 402, 422.
   He does repeat the purchasing power assumption in III, III, where he is discussing the difficulties in empirical determinations of demand, – a reasonable repetition under these circumstances. Note his easy dismissal: "this difficulty can however be overcome fairly well" whereas you are still unwilling to define your interpretation explicitly.

3. The alternative possibility is that the average price of non-rival goods be held constant. This you dismiss (on what I think is a peculiar ground, – that it is non-rigorous: what of his capital concept, his avoidance of stationary conditions and perfect competition, his representative firm, etc.?) I have a feeling that in a pure mood he would take this interpretation, in a "realistic" mood no. 1 above.

4.   I wish you would reflect upon the state of the theory of index numbers, and of the available information, in the 1870's and 1880's. Then I wish you'd explain how Marshall could think that it was easy to allow for changes in the purchasing power of money, and whether he was likely to devise a theory whose application to real problems was contingent upon unavailable statistics and perhaps theory.

I'll read your article carefully in Canada and send you some detailed comments. In a way you are losing the argument to the critics: even if you retain your view, you are presenting it so defensively, so subtly, and seizing so eagerly upon thin threads of argument, that it will not carry conviction to the general reader. For this reason, if no other, you ought to put it on ice for quite a period and then rewrite it.

There is no news here. I'm finishing up my education piece,[218] and taking much more work than I should to Canada. I hope to read Gossen and Dupuit,[219] do some work on my text,[220] read Mitchell's lectures,[221] etc., to say nothing of leading a vigorous outdoor life.

Regards

George

July 10 [1948]

Dear Milt:

Like the stubborn men we are, I am carried away with admiration for the industry and analytical skill the Marshall paper displays, but am not ready to accept it. I have nothing to add on my last letter in general, but perhaps I will after I've done some reading this fall.

However, here are a few specific comments:

p. 2: why is exegesis unrewarding and inconclusive?
p. 3: Couldn't this mean same over time, in statistical studies?
pp. 4–12: the footnotes drown out the text, and leave a rather confused picture in the reader's mind. Can't you segregate all the historical stuff and give it chronologically?
p. 13: the redundancy of (5) arises because you list it as equal to (1) – (4).
p. 22: paragraph a. isn't very informative.
p. 24: This is really crucial: you've got to show explicitly that your interpretation is useful. Exactly how does it handle a shift of demand (presumably tastes); can you even define your demand curve then?
Incidentally, should you note that after 1895 M. deleted the statement, "one universal law of demand"?
p. 35: Are you implying that there was no tradition of demand curve analysis before 1890? How about Cournot?[222] – with whom M. was familiar.
p. 37: Illustrate the logically inconsistent statements.
p. 39: we curtsy to M, for pay lip service?

We are all settled and I have been doing a lot of chores. The family is all fine, and living in the lake.

Regards

George
Windermere
Ontario

I just got an AER article by Gramp[223] on rent controls; he had the nerve to use <u>your</u> D[emand] curve.

July 26 [1948]

Dear Milt

I haven't even the 5th ed. of Marshall so I cannot give an independent assessment of note II. It always bothered me a little, but I had a different, and fuzzy, interpretation. I am prepared to believe that he had some funny twists in his brain on this subject; your interpretation still does not seem one of those illuminating strokes of jig-saw solution.

My only (!) objection to the first part of your appendix is that it is question-begging. On a literal interpretation, both interpretations fail. So you modify yours to fit. Why not the current interpretation: for example, by interpreting "indefinitely great" as relative to money income; or by introducing wealth for this "emergency" situation.

I agree that this is an excellent time to write the essay – you have all the dope at your finger tips. I think it is a bad time to publish, in the flush of discovery and controversy. I find it hard to imagine a reason for haste in publishing, from your viewpoint. By December I'll agree with you or convince you that you're wrong.

Many thanks for the comments on the education essay.[224] I'll work on all of them, altho trying to find excuses for avoiding your major suggestion.

The two older boys are now swimming pretty well – I'm in the water so much helping them that even I am becoming a fair swimmer! Jerry goes in whenever the mood hits, with or without clothes, and likes to jump off the dock. I've been reading Gossen,[225] and find him more interesting than I thought possible.

Regards,

George

[September, 1948]

Dear Milt:

I am a weary housewife, but still have enough energy to write a confused letter. Two weeks ago we left Canada and stopped the first night at
Greensburg, Pa., to visit Chick's brother for a day. Jerry started running a
temperature and went to the hospital with inflamed ears. An X-ray then
revealed pneumonia, and he is still in the hospital, mending but slowly –
it's virus, and not amenable to penicillin. I left with the boys 10 days ago
to start them in school, and have been holding down the fort with the boys
– and the neighbor's help – since. I hope that Chick and Jerry will get back
by the end of this week.

Your utility article is splendid in its revision.[226] I'm amazed at the thor-
oughness with which you revised the first draft. Can you spare say 5
reprints so my students can work on it?

On Marshall, I've done a little reading and would like your comments
on the following:

1. Edgeworth's article on demand curves in Palgrave's Dictionary,[227]
   which surely reached Marshall's notice but was not, I'd guess, revised
   on the critical point (in my favor) in later editions.
2. In the pure theory of domestic values,[228] Marshall gives a definition of
   the price axis, p. 3, that would be ambiguous on your interpretation.
   See also p. 15.
3. How can the Friedman demand curves of different individuals be
   added? Since the individuals use different quantities of various goods,
   there must be different compensating changes in other prices, so the
   functions will not have common arguments. Yet Marshall added the
   demand curves of different classes.
4. Marshall says purchasing power pertains to the country and not to the
   individual (Memorials, p. 207[229]).
5. Principles, p. 109, to cite again: "The purchasing power of money is
   continually changing,...." This is sensible as an observation on a Fisher
   P; it is less obviously valid in discussing reaction of quantity of sugar to
   price. And when he says that the Broader Changes can be measured
   roughly, again he must have a cost of living index in mind. For surely
   the variations appropriate to sugar, etc. price fluctuations are small, and
   hence he has an unemployable technical apparatus on your reading.

On the methodology, I'll also think some more. Personally I would like
it published[230] (in part because I've paraphrased the argument in two para-

graphs of my Chamberlin essay,[231] and would like to give a more specific reference). But I keep feeling that you arouse skepticism and opposition by stopping where you do. Because surely in some sense an assumption can be more promising than another. If I predict basing points in industries where the geographical pattern of consumption is unstable, you (I hope) will find this worth looking into. If I predict basing points in industries where Yale men are over Princeton men, and love to rib Fetter's[232] disciples, you sneer, although you haven't a shred of evidence that the latter is inferior in predictive value to the former. It is surely possible to say something about some assumptions being more promising than others, and yet not to take back any of the things you are saying at present. If you can pierce this muddy frontier of your article, it would be a great improvement. (An alternative way of arguing this is: if we really could devise good theories only by theorizing and then testing against predictions, good theories would be chance events, as likely to come from Seymour Harris – no more likely, – than from Smith or Marshall. Only an infinitesimal portion of scientific work would be rewarding. And I don't believe this.)

Arthur, I've just heard from Moore,[233] wants me to write another service industry monograph. It will be interesting to see whether I can be overpowered.

Regards,

George

October 4, 1948

Prof. George J. Stigler
Department of Economics
Fayerweather Hall
Columbia University
New York, N. Y.

Dear George:

You certainly do have rotten luck. You have my sympathy for your experience with Jerry. I trust he's all better now, and that Chick and he are back with you.

I have sent you some reprints of the utility article,[234] though I don't know whether I would recommend that you have your students work on it.

I haven't really had a chance to look up your references on Marshall. We got back just a little over a week ago, and what with classes getting started this week, getting fixed up at home, Rose and I both getting colds, I really haven't done very much else.

However, your comments leave me confused as to what you think my interpretation of Marshall is. I am not pretending to argue that Marshall is interpreting the demand curve in such a way as to exclude the Hicksian income effect completely. I am merely arguing that he held the purchasing power of money in the market sense constant. The argument is that if one holds the same such basic other things as the total quantity of money and people's desires for real balances, then any decline or rise in one price must be associated with such a change in other prices as to keep a particular index of purchasing power of money unchanged. On this interpretation I don't see any difficulty at all in adding the demand curves of individuals. The question is, what would be the quantity purchased by Mr. A or Mr. B or Mr. C if the price of sugar were such and such, and the price index number such and such. That's a straightforward objective question, and I don't see why it raises any difficulty in adding demand curves of different individuals. This fits in with your comment that Marshall says that purchasing power pertains to the country and not to the individual. I think it does in the sense in which he was using it. I think he was interested in individual demand curves primarily as a basis for market demand curves.

I shall have to postpone comment on your comment on Edgeworth and on Marshall's pure theory of domestic values.

I think part of the difficulty you have on the methodology problem arises out of the fact that the issues it deals with pertain only to one small part of all work in economics. One might, I suppose, separate out four kinds of things that economists and other scientists do: first, the collection of data to provide something to generalize from; second, the derivation of hypotheses to generalize the empirical uniformities discovered in the data; third, the testing of these hypotheses; and fourth, the utilization of them. My strictures apply only to the third of these steps. Clearly in the process of collecting data to be generalized, realism and respect for detail, and so on, are all to the good. The real problem that you raise arises, I take it, when somebody has proposed a theory which we haven't as yet been able to test, and the question arises, shall we use it instead of some alternative. It's at this point that one is most likely to say that he is judging the theory by its assumption and to say that he will have some confidence in it if the assumptions are reasonable, and he will not if they are not. This is the kind of point Arthur was raising most strenuously this summer against it. I'm inclined to argue that the logical counterpart of the intuitive process whereby we reach such judgments is a process of indirect testing, that our so-called theories are not separate, concrete, disparate things, but fit together into some kind of a whole. And what is involved is that we have certain phases of our theory in which we have a good deal of confidence because they have stood the test of experience, that certain kinds of assumptions or kinds of theories have in those fields turned out better than others, and that that's the real basis for our confidence in one theory or another. Thus, to take your example, we would be unlikely to have much confidence in predictions made that basing points will arise in industries where Yale men are over Princeton men simply because that kind of a theory, that kind of a set of assumptions, isn't one with which we've had very good luck in the past. We don't have any tested segment of economic theory which uses that kind of data. On the other hand, we might be interested in a theory that basing points will arise when the geographical pattern of consumption is unstable, because that does tie in with some other elements of our theory that seems to yield correct results. This is all very hazy and sketchy but it seems to me to suggest the direction in which one wants to go.

Look at the question from another angle. You say if we really could devise good theories only by theorizing and then testing against predictions, good theories would be chance events. I don't believe that follows at all. We want theories about <u>something</u> and certainly whether we will have a good theory or not depends on what it is that the theory is designed to generalize. The discovery of empirical regularities is not theorizing, and yet is there any doubt but that it provides a basis for theorizing and that it will greatly affect the validity of the theorizing that's done? A theory constructed to generalize alleged facts that are incorrect is so much wasted effort. Now, collection of data on empirical regularities occurs implicitly and internally as well as through objective data collecting. What really, it seems to me, distinguishes Smith and Marshall, the two examples you cite, is that both of them were very thorough empirical workers, and did a good job of systematizing the empirical data they observed, extracting from them empirical regularities, and then providing generalizations for these empirical regularities.

Best regards to the family,

Yours,

Milton Friedman

MF:rm

[October, 1948]

Dear Milt:

Life continues on a steady keel: Steve broke his arm in a fall Sunday (not serious), and my sinuses are kicking up! At present my intellectual life is wrapped up in teachers' salaries,[235] which I hope to finish up in a couple of weeks, but I'll try to draw myself up to your abstract interests.

Re Marshall, your ms. (p. 13)[236] certainly implies a trivial or zero income effect for the individual on the Friedman interpretation of the demand curve of the individual. But ignoring your phrasing, isn't there a real problem? If I ever want to break up the market demand curve (say for a study of price discrimination), you are asking me to do what seems a strange and purposeless thing, namely, study variations of quantity with price in the parts of the market, on the assumption that other prices change in a way that keeps the real income of the combined parts more or less steady.

Re methodology,[237] I may be misinterpreted a little. I like your general position but want you to enlarge it, – precisely as you are enlarging it in your letter to me. While some elaboration along these lines will take some of the paradox out of your thesis (and in a certain sense weaken its message unless you write very carefully), it will create sympathy for and receptiveness to your thesis and make the paper much more influential.

Wolman[238] tells me – confidentially – that Hayek[239] wants a professorship here (US), possibly Princeton. Apparently some deal was approached to the Institute,[240] but they shied away from the funds tied to it (Foundation?).

I am still holding out on Arthur[241] on the service industries.[242] Part of my resistance is no doubt irrational: that the NB[243] is trying to liquidate a past commitment to the Falk[244] people. But I think Arthur is going on the basis that I really haven't any deeply felt desire to work another field, which may be true; however I do have a desire not to work the services. So I intend to spurn it, and begin my oligopoly explorations[245] (after I write up the basing point system).[246]

Columbia is now looking for a European Institute economist, and for a Far Eastern Institute economist – would that we were allowed to look for a good economist.

George

November 8, 1948

Mr. George J. Stigler
4 Farley Road
Scarsdale, New York

Dear George:

Just a note to say I am going to be in New York from the 20th through the 23rd of November. I am meeting with Al Hart and Emile Despres (the committee on economic stability)[247] on Saturday and Sunday. I am staying over on Monday and Tuesday for Bureau work, and sometime during the period I hope we can get together. I'll call you when I get in.

Sincerely yours,

Milton Friedman

MF:rm

[December 1948]

Dear Milt:

I was glad to hear you are writing on Mitchell qua theorist,[248] and hasten to ask you some questions (and, of course, give the answers).

I recently reread the *Backward Art of Spending Money*,[249] and on reflection decided its author was the most dogmatic theorist I had ever encountered: he was telling housewives to behave like entrepreneurs. And Mitchell had said he loved theory, in that famous letter to J. M. Clark.[250] Could it be that he fought theory so violently in order to convince himself?

Or, alternatively, if a pure scientist – one believing only demonstrated things – is asked his opinion on policy, he must decline to answer – and listen to his intellectual inferiors give advice on policy. Hence the role of the pure scientist is terribly painful to assume in economics. Your fiscal article,[251] my minimum wages,[252] all of Henry Simons are impure science, and verboten. Can you mention a single instance of written advice on specific policy from Mitchell?

Or, again, if one loves theory but doesn't believe it is valid, is not the study of the history of doctrine the only respectable method of catering to the love? And why else did Mitchell cultivate this field so assiduously?

The memorial services were very good.[253] Of the many speakers only one was terrible – shallow and pretentious. Joe Schumpeter.[254]

I may be seeing you soon – I want to clear up the NB[255] thing before I write to Aaron,[256] however.

Regards

George

[January, 1949]

Dear Milt

Before I forget it, you ought to look at the last chapter of Hardy's *Risk and Risk Bearing*[257] – it contains an absurd argument that gambling is economically rational.

I have been beating my brains out on the basing points without coming to grips with anything interesting. Almost everything I touch turns to dust – thus Fetter's allegations of basing points in copper[258] (which I wouldn't expect because most of the consumers are in the Connecticut Valley) may be simply a confusing of the most common method of quotation (N.Y. refinery, where the overwhelming majority of the refineries are). About the only thing I learned, and should have known, is that a cartel is also silly: they are forced to use basing points because the individual firms will not give up their personal contacts (because the cartel may fold).

I don't understand your objection to my statement on cross-hauling. I say that if personal connections are necessary (perhaps because of technical consultations of producers and buyers) a firm must plan to make sales in other areas at all times, and not merely when its own area is in a low state, and this is demonstrable from the steel case. One might say that it's cheaper to cross-haul steel than salesmen.

Rumor has it that Samuelson was quite the unsuccessful suave chairman, a la Schumpeter,[259] at the meetings.[260] Sol[omon] Fabricant said he referred to you as an altar boy or something of the sort; I would have relished being there to see your reaction. It may merely be prejudice, but I'm inclined to write him off as an economist. Two of his recent jobs (the Survey article[261] and his essay in the Hansen festshrift[262]) were pure mathematical exposition, as is also his current *Economica* item[263] (which, by the way, has already been done better by Wold),[264] and his textbook[265] suggests that he doesn't know anything that hasn't appeared in the *Survey of Current Business*.

All is quiet and well in our household. I've started to teach Steve equations and it goes pretty well but I wish I could find a book for the job.

Regards

George

January 26, 1949

(This is not my idea, I need hardly add. I'm prepared to reprint your work & mine.)

Professor Milton Friedman
University of Chicago
Chicago, Illinois

Dear Friedman:

Kenneth Boulding and I are to edit the American Economic Association's volume of readings in price theory,[266] and at this preliminary stage we wish to solicit your advice on its scope. Thereafter it will be possible to compile a bibliography and do some preliminary screening, and we hope we may then call on you again for advice on the specific contents.

Price theory can be made to embrace almost every branch of economic theory, but it is conventionally interpreted to embrace utility and demand, costs and pricing, and perhaps distribution. The doubtful areas are:

1. Welfare and "socialist" economics
2. Economic dynamics
3. Distribution
4. Empirical studies and studies of empirical methodology (illustrated by say articles on the supply curve of labor and on statistical demand curves, respectively).

The second and third topics are already partly covered in the readings on business cycles and income distribution, of course. If the first or fourth topic is deemed very important, it should probably be left for a later volume. One way of indicating your preferences on coverage concretely would be to name three or four articles at whose omission you would complain.

In addition there is another type of question of scope:

5. Should only recent articles be included, or is it permissible or desirable to go back twenty or forty years?
6. Should the practice of reprinting only journal articles be continued, or should selections from books also be considered?

We shall appreciate your opinions – and those of your colleagues – on these and any other points that may occur to you.

Sincerely yours,

George Stigler

GS:ES

February 22, 1949

Professor George J. Stigler
Department of Economics
Columbia University
New York 27, New York

Dear George:

This is in reply to your letter of January 26 written of behalf of you and Kenneth Boulding and raising certain questions about the American Economic Association's volume of readings in price theory.[267]

As to the scope of the volume, it seems clear to me that distribution should definitely be included under price theory. I am also inclined to argue that some material under your heading four should also be included. The line to draw here is between studies or articles about empirical work that are of interest primarily for substantive conclusions they contain and studies or articles that are of interest primarily for their discussion of concepts on which the statistician is to work or for their discussion of the implications of the statistical work for theoretical constructs. To illustrate I think E.J. Working's article on "What Do Statistical Demand Curves Show?" in the *Quarterly Journal of Economics* for 1927 is an article that would well deserve reprinting. It deals with the problems of statistical demand curves but in the process it has a good deal to say indirectly about the theoretical concepts involved. I doubt that there are very many articles of this kind that you would want to include but there might be two or three. I am somewhat more dubious about welfare and "socialist" economics. Again there are some articles of this character such as some of Lange's[268] which really are exercises in economic theory and there might be something to be said for reprinting some of these. On the whole I should be less inclined to include items under your heading one than under your heading four.

With respect to your question five, I think that it would be highly desirable to go back twenty, forty or for that matter a hundred years if the article of that date seemed the best treatment of a particular topic. In general it seems to me the criterion ought to be to get the article that is best, regardless of date. With respect to question six, I think selections from books as well as general articles should be considered. Of course, it would be absurd to include selections from the classics that every graduate student of economics ought to be expected to read at some time or another, so there would be little point of including selections from Marshall, Ricardo, Smith and the like. On the other hand there would be a good deal to be said to include selections from books that are of a very much less widely known, or in which the theoretical material is a small part of the whole. For example, there is material in Wicksteed's *Common Sense of Political Economy*[269] that could stand reprinting and surely in books of recent years, especially various specialized monographs there will be found parts that may be relevant.

Sincerely yours,

Milton Friedman

MF:sb

April 25 [1949]

Dear Milt

Letters are crossing each other at a great rate, and this may be no exception.

My interpretation of your position – in the other letter – seems to be approximately correct. I do warn the reader that the matter is controversial, by the reference to you and by phrases such as "I interpret $\underline{I}$ in Marshall's equation. . ." The question is: is this enough warning? Or should I – if I understand your view – point out the alternative interpretation of note II, or of the statement of the constancy of the marginal utility of income. But then, why don't I present my objections to your interpretation?

But I am writing a history of utility theory as I see it, not an essay on Marshall.[270] Look at my problem. I disagree with parts of Mitchell on Bentham,[271] with Robbins on Menger,[272] with Wicksell on Launhardt,[273] with Schumpeter on Fisher,[274] etc etc. I cannot believe it is my duty to criticize or refute these interpretations, or yours.

I do not think your interpretation is foolish, or I would not have spent so much time on it. But I do think I must treat Marshall briefly or I destroy the concept of the paper. And I know I cannot refute your views – if I can then – without taking a considerable amount of space. Which I have no intention of doing. Is this position unreasonable?

We shall definitely expect you in NY on the 11th.

Regards

George

PS
Tell Janet[275] she is wrong – a child outlives several generations of toys.

[May 1949]

Dear Milt

I have read the WCM piece[276] and I'm returning parts of it. I hope to read the theory section of the 1913 volume,[277] so I'm keeping this part in the hope that I may learn enough to be able to make useful remarks.

My general reaction is that it is a fine bold piece, and should it be? As you say, one likes a theory that cuts in to the heart of the matter and willfully disregards the nonessentials and trimmings. But can one do this in writing history of doctrine? Partly yes, but partly also no. I think one should pay more attention to the qualifications and the shadings to avoid the charge of having read ones own interpretation into the work. Many of my suggestions are essentially along this line.

We have already discussed some of the general points, like the division into types of economic theory. In some ways I prefer the division: statics (no process problem); fluctuations (no non-process problem); and long-run development (no theory). In general I think you should tone down the claims for the theory of relative prices, and perhaps also those for the non-process theory of money.

> p. 8: Is it obvious that an instinctive use of neoclassical monetary theory would have helped in constructing a general theory of fluctuations?
> p. 10: You get in trouble with this enumeration. It would be sufficient to say that the 19th century paid relatively little attention to the problem.
> p. 14: Here and elsewhere I worry that you overplay the historian. Incidentally, is it possible to study the cycle empirically without engaging in the study of economic history as you use the term?
> p. 20: Same thing. I bet Mitchell's history is not as good as Heckscher's history of mercantilism.[278]

I might say that I have a much lower opinion of Mitchell as a historian. His lectures[279] reveal no critical or independent study. If we finesse the first two books,[280] and start with 1913, have you any evidence for the historical bent?

> p. 28: You claim too much for the lectures. They show that some important issues in theory were related to some important contemporary developments, and no more. I, for one, do not even fully understand why Malthus[281] was accepted; I should think the capitalists would have enjoyed an optimistic theory even more.

p. 30: I don't see how one could positively demonstrate that disturbing causes do not bring about the cycle. No casual enumeration from the infinite number of events can be even remotely persuasive, especially since one does not know – in the absence of a theory – the importance to attribute to each event. I should argue that it is the fundamental teleology of science that this kind of theory is the denial of theory.

p. 35: Malthus' population moved in cycles.

p. 57: Is there an analytical distinction between building on previous work and redoing it in a better fashion? Was it wrong to determine the gravitational constant to another decimal place?

As I said, I shall write to you about the cycle theory if I get to learn anything about it. I have a feeling that you are simplifying Mitchell's theory. If it can be expressed in terms of a fairly short list of functions, why did not Hansen[282] (Minnesota Hansen) or Robertson[283] or someone like that do it before? I conjecture that you have pulled out one of several possible theories. If there is any basis for this conjecture, and even if there isn't, might it not be desirable to put the notes in an appendix? This will reduce the suspicion that you are putting the theory in Mitchell, however unfounded that suspicion may be. In some ways, indeed, it would fit M's attitude better if the notes began: M. was adverse to strict formal theories, and he did not know enough – he believed – to decide on one of several variants, or possibly believed that each variant had its role, and I select the following model only because it was clearly present and shows the complexity of the model with which he dealt. Perhaps this is wholly wrong, but I offer it for what it is worth.

We're finally winding up here. Classes end tomorrow, exams in about 2 weeks. I have high hopes of getting off to Canada about June 15 or 20. I seem to get more tired of economics each spring, which I guess is due to the fact that the next fall I forget I'm getting older. I'm also horrified by how easy it is to get into activities that once I used to think would be wonderful. I think I'll set a rule. No activity under $500 because it's too costly; none over $501 because its immoral – and watch the figure rise.

Regards,

George

Dec 5 [1949]

Dear Milt

In the third edition of the Principles[284] (p. 606) Marshall talks of workers' surplus and savers' surplus – in each case a sort of rent. He adds the note

> Consumers' surplus has relation in the first instance to individual commodities, and each part of it responds directly to changes in the conjuncture affecting the terms on which that commodity is to be had: while the two kinds of producer's surplus appear always in terms of the general return that the conjuncture gives a certain amount of purchasing power. (p. 831 of 8th edition[285])

Does this not put you in the position of saying that by 1895 M[arshall] was not merely confused, but almost explicitly denied your interpretation?

I'm sending along the remainder of my draft soon.[286] I've decided to leave it anti-Friedman until I've read your article, thought, read, and argued.

See you soon

George

P.S. Math. Note XIV also has some troublesome phrases.

[December, 1949]

Dear Milt:

I am enclosing the remaining portions of my history.[287] You will see that I continue the orthodox interpretation of Marshall.

It was written before I read the article,[288] which is really an extraordinary performance: whether you are right or wrong, it is wonderful to have found a new interpretation of this well-worked material. I still adhere to the orthodox view, and as defense attach a quotation from M.[289] explicitly stating that demand curves do not represent equal utilities at all points. I could supplement this defense, but you deserve a rest from this subject, and for the time I shall merely assert that M. was not as good as you believe.

      Regards,

      George

Though not of great practical importance, the case of multiple positions of (stable) equilibrium offers a good illustration of the error involved in the doctrine of maximum satisfaction when stated as a universal truth. For the position in which a small amount is produced and sold at a high price would be the first to be reached, and when reached would be regarded according to that doctrine as that which gave the absolute maximum of aggregate satisfaction. But another position of equilibrium corresponding to a larger production and a lower price would be equally satisfactory to the producers, and would be <u>much more satisfactory to the consumers</u>; the excess of Consumers' Rent in the second case over the first would represent the increase in aggregate satisfaction. (1st ed., p. 451–2, n.) (8th ed., p. 472n)

[January, 1950]

Dear Milt

I envy you, for you have not had two weeks between terms in which you accomplished nothing.

You will be amazed to hear that Noyes[290] congratulated me on my dispassionate discussion of professors' salaries.[291] And less so to hear that Don Wallace thinks my treatment of school teachers intolerably below the level of Bureau Work – the idea, comparing them with office workers. I can't say I've been pleased with Arthur's[292] and Geoff's[293] reaction: I should make only comparisons between college trained girls in various occupations, or failing that, make some comparisons in which teachers are not highest. I have concocted a duller text and a sharper table and shall see how it goes. Nobody will answer my question: why should a lower level of precision be tolerated everywhere else in the report than at this one point?

Have you read the UN report of the experts on full employment?[294] It's dreadful. Why don't you suggest a review article – Lutz[295] could do a good job.*

I am revising my history of utility theory so you had better complain soon. I am occasionally heroic – I took out Senior, Lloyd, and Jennings[296] – but keep adding elsewhere so Hamilton[297] will swoon when he sees it.

Ask Rose if it is possible to start mimeographing the bibliography now, even if compilation is not complete.[298] I'm averaging a letter a week from Blakiston[299] and Haley[300] and eventually they will penetrate my turgid replies.

Frankie[301] was here two days ago, much in a dither. I haven't had any good ideas for a program yet. He's hep on methodology: would you be interested in giving a paper? It would be fascinating to the audience to hear your heresies, and would require no work of you. What do you think of my talking – not that I want to give a paper at all – on the logic of the study of the history of economics? I could finish up my paper on the division of labor and the extent of the market, but it is more relevant to the theory of economic development than to the kind of thing Frankie has in mind.

I just got your comments. Some points like the convexity conditions I had caught, and the others I had not. I shall certainly accept the suggestion of careful reworking: Perhaps I was wrong in choosing to write on utility on which I know little and care little.[302]

The only point on a first skimming where I'm tentatively adamant is on the constancy of the marginal utility of money. I don't see why its coming much later is decisive, altho it should be noted. I was seeking a way to get to $x = f(p_x)$ from $U_x = g(x)$ – and perhaps I shouldn't; you of course go to $x = f(P_x, P_y \ldots)$

I guess I'll put in references to contemporary work after all – my studied policy not to was of course the reason you were not in. I wanted to avoid cluttering the story with private quarrels which did not come in the period surveyed, but this is probably no reason for leaving out references too.

Regards,

George

* I hear that almost any ex-ECA[303] man can write a scandalous article on British policies of the last few years.

[February, 1950]

Dear Milt

I enclose a new version of Marshall,[304] which you are naturally expected to use as the basis for your future class-room discussions. It seems crucial now how one interprets the statement (Bk III, Ch. 3): "the marginal utility . . . is a fixed quantity." You say it is an identity; I that it is an assumption. I accepted your view as long as I read the passage in the light of what followed, but I now think it must be read in the light of what precedes. I am also impressed by the fact that if it is not an assumption, then where in Bk III will we find it – and we both agree it is essential to consumer surplus. It would be intolerable for Marshall to state it only in the mathematical appendix.

I am plodding through the rest of the revision slowly, and have drafted an entirely new conclusion.

Arthur[305] says he's coming out to Chicago soon for a visit. His annual report[306] is an elegant performance.

Did you know Slutsky[307] died in 1948? I've asked Homan[308] to ask Marschak[309] to write a note on him – there are Russian obituaries by Komolgoroff and Smirnov.[310] I read the latter with some care and finally deduced from the title that Slutsky was 68 years old.

Regards,

George

PS

In the enclosure, numbers in brackets are corresponding 8th edition pagination.

PST

I have finally reached an understanding of Ricardo,[311] and I'm impressed by the analogy to the difficulty in understanding Marshall. As long as I tried to understand only the meaning of Ricardo's individual sentences he seemed preposterously illogical, as all the notes I made in the margin when I was a graduate student remind me. Only when I quit arguing every step with him did I see the structure – and a crazy, wonderful structure it is.

February 27, 1950

Professor George J. Stigler
Department of Economics
Columbia University
New York, New York

Dear George:

Re Marshall's treatment of consumer's surplus and constancy of the marginal utility of money, let me cite the following:
(1). In 1ˢᵗ edition, page 175, footnote 1:³¹² "The following account of Consumers' Rent is reproduced with slight alterations from some papers printed for private circulation in 1879." Comparison will show that the alterations (up to page 178 and inclusive of footnote on page 177) are indeed slight. Now in the <u>Pure Theory</u>,³¹³ the word utility is used occasionally but there is no real utility analysis, and there is no hint that Marshall recognized the problem that is raised by changes in the marginal utility of money – in terms of my Figure 1, there is no evidence that he recognized the difference between Aa and CV. His utility analysis was apparently developed later and is incorporated in Note VI of the Math Appendix. However, in incorporating the discussion of the <u>Pure Theory</u> into the Principles he neglected to make the necessary qualification about small fraction of expenditures on the commodity.
(2). The alternative interpretation, that he did not make the qualification here because he had already made it earlier, is rendered questionable by the second edition [1891]. In that edition, the above footnote is omitted, and on page 182 a footnote is inserted reading, "It is not necessary for our present purpose to take account of the possibility that the marginal utility of money to him might be appreciably altered in the course of his purchases." The inclusion of the explicit qualification in a text almost unchanged otherwise, argues that he did not consider it covered earlier. The words "for our present purpose" argues strongly that he did not intend constant marginal utility of money to apply to his entire analysis including the earlier demand curve. From the second edition on, the qualification is included explicitly in the consumer surplus discussion.
(3). In the course of looking this material up, I stumbled across footnote 1, page 126 (8ᵗʰ edition [1920]), first two paragraphs, first introduced in 3ʳᵈ edition. As an aside – does it support my interpretation of Marshall, or yours?
(4). Re "the marginal utility . . . is a fixed quantity" (Book III, Chapter 3), I believe the above disposes of any need to interpret it as an assumption in order to have it in the text for the consumer surplus discussion. So let us

look at it in its own right. The first edition seems to me clearest on this. And here the evidence that I find most persuasive is the extent to which the text is a literal translation of Mathematical notes II and III. For brevity, let me number the sentences in the text, beginning with the sentence at the bottom of page 155 (1ˢᵗ edition), "If we take a man as he is...", 1, 2, etc; and number the sentences in the Math. App., beginning with Note II, a (all of Note II), b, ... Note the correspondence and exactness of translation:

Sentences in Text	Translation of
(1), (2)	(a)
(3)	(b)
(4)	(c), (d)
(5), prior to semicolon	(e)
(5), after semicolon)	(f), (g)
(6))	

The preceding paragraph (containing (1), (2)) has a footnote reference to Note II, the paragraph containing (3) through (6) to Note III. These two notes together follow precisely the same order as the text, yet they nowhere say anything that you could even remotely interpret as requiring or implying constancy of the marginal utility of money, except in the sense of an identity. Thus Marshall's textual order cannot be said to require this.

Furthermore, with respect to your contention that Marshall wants constant marginal utility of money so that he can use the equation [GAP HERE] (page 737) as a means of translating the utility curve into a demand curve, note that he explicitly refuses an opportunity to do that in Math. Note III. Surely if that were what he wanted to do, he would have done so at the bottom of page 737 immediately after giving the above equation. And it would have been entirely unnecessary to have gone on to consider other commodities and to derive the second equation on page 738. Moreover he would have written the above equation: [GAP HERE]. Instead, he deliberately eschews this and proceeds by the more roundabout way of eliminating [GAP HERE]. Why does he introduce it [GAP HERE] at all? This is fairly clear from page 738. He does it to enable himself to prove, through supposedly obvious proposition in sentence (e) – diminishing marginal utility of money – the propositions in (f) and (g). Note that he starts the final paragraph of Note III with a "Therefore." In other words, instead of introducing [GAP HERE] to hold it constant, he introduces it precisely in order to use changes in it to establish propositions about the effect of various variables on the marginal demand price. And this, of course, holds equally for his textual discussion.

Note also that on page 156, after completing the translation of Notes II and III, he returns to the notion of distributing money among different uses so that the marginal utility per penny's worth will be the same in different uses. The final paragraph of Section 6 reiterates what I take to have been the purpose of what precedes, namely that he is showing how you can calculate the marginal demand price for a particular quantity and what relation it has to utility. That is, all that precedes is devoted to explaining what underlies a particular point on a demand curve; what it is that determines the demand price for a particular quantity, and what will raise or lower the demand price. Section 7 then goes on to get the demand schedule by saying that you can put many of these points together. On your logic, the place where constant marginal utility of money is needed is between Section 6 and 7, not in Section 5.

In the second edition, the statement "let us translate this law of diminishing utility into terms of price," is explicitly <u>not</u> to be interpreted as "let us translate this law of d. u." into a "demand curve." It is again, as in the first edition, a means of investigating the factors bearing on the marginal demand price. And he uses diminishing utility in this analysis. On your interpretation of it Section 4 in the 2nd edition (p. 153) is gibberish, since he has already done what he now sets out to do. On your interpretation, his knowledge of the demand schedule is complete, and "To complete our knowledge of his demand for it" not a task that remains. On mine, what precedes explains but one point on the demand curve.

(5). In my earlier comments on recognizing Knight and me,[314] I did not have reference to inclusion of footnote references, but rather to recognition that "the demand curve" cannot be taken to be a self-evident thing but must be defined precisely and explicitly.

Sincerely yours,

Milton Friedman

MF/gj

[March, 1950]

Dear Milt

I had not intended to stimulate you to new work on Marshall, but I am glad to get the new material and criticisms.

Your criticisms and elaboration have convinced me, in a way I wasn't really convinced before, of the deep ambiguity in M., and of the fact that no interpretation is going to fit all of his writings. I can now see how, once your interpretation is accepted, one can find comfort and support at many places.

I've come to the conclusion that no economic theory is important unless one's contemporaries are persuaded to adopt it. If it meets this test, it is important; if it does not, it is unimportant – no matter how correct or profound it may be. From this view it is quite unimportant whether M. had your theory, since no one saw it. And still from this viewpoint, your task is to persuade economists of its usefulness. You have done some of this in your article,[315] but my guess is that you must do more to deflect so powerful a current of thought as you oppose. I am also in doubt whether you should ever have associated the theory with Marshall – even granting that you are wholly correct. What you gain by his authority (which I'd guess is not an awful lot) you lose by introducing a controversial question of interpretation that inevitably deflects attention from your main thesis.

And now I promise not to speak of M. to you again for a time. You must be bored with him by now, and deserve a rest.

Life has its usual jolts here. I may have told you that we learned that Chick's dad had a bad a case of TB. So everyone (16) who had been to Canada was x-rayed, and our Jerry was the only loser. He must stay in bed 3 to 6 months. He feels fine, and seems to be progressing nicely, and the MDs assure us that he will make a complete recovery. But still I could do without it. Don't tell anyone. He's not contagious but for small reasons the MD recommended that we keep quiet about it.

Regards

George

March 27 [1950]

Dear Milt

I had already grown to dislike that excise-income tax, and I admit its error.[316] I also agree to the desirability of keeping the quantity of resources in mind, although it is an open question whether this should be done through demand curve analysis.

Since you requested it, I started to list several crucial difficulties in your Marshallian article,[317] and then decided that they can wait a year or two. I would suggest, wholly disregarding Marshall, that if you do more work on this, one subject should be the detailed analysis of whose income is to be held constant, and how the economist can hold it constant.

Incidentally, I'm taking up Marshall in the history of thought. I'm taking the untenable position that he is perfect at every point, and I'm horrified by how feebly the students attack it.

I enclose a quote designed to enrich your future discussions of advertising.

I'm going down to Washington Friday to talk to Levi;[318] I have some misgivings about an appearance, especially in light of that vicious Joint Committee proposal.

Tell Rose I'm panting for bibliography.[319]

Regards,

George

[Spring 1950]

Dear Milt

When you write that you are shocked with my treatment of Marshall,[320] I suspect that there has been no meeting of the minds. I know you do not mean that I disagree with your interpretation, and I assume that you do not mean that I have failed to give a more or less coherent account on the conventional interpretation. So I infer that you believe a satisfactory discussion of Marshall will take account of many passages and points which you have raised in your article and letters. If this inference is correct, I disagree with it.

Since I adhere to the conventional interpretation, Marshall is a minor figure in the history of utility theory. Hence I have no right to discuss details of his exposition at length; this would involve injustice to every other author I study. If I accepted your interpretation, I still would not enter into the structure of the much debated "translation of diminishing utility into price," etc. I would then, (1) state my acceptance of your view, (2) briefly state why, and (3) proceed with the conventional exposition because that is the interpretation that is important in the history of utility during Marshall's life. On neither view would I properly discuss the many detailed points and issues you raise.

This matter of my treatment has nothing to do with something you have a full right to expect: a careful and sympathetic study of your article[321] and letters. I have certainly tried to fulfill this expectation, although I have not written to you for a year on why this study has not changed my mind. Perhaps this was wrong in conveying an impression of imperviousness to your arguments; it was done because (i) the months immediately after publication are a hell of a time to ask you to change your mind, and (ii) the scientific importance of what Marshall meant is not sufficient to justify arousing you to further work on him.

If I have not made the correct inference on your position, or if my reply to it is unconvincing, please tell me.

Incidentally, I hope you understand that I want you to be right. If you are right, it is a very pretty triumph over the field. Since I will be wrong with everyone else, it will be no personal reflection on me. So our vested interests are identical.

I find it possible to contain my admiration for Hamilton[322] in this matter. To say my exposition was not influenced by your article is shallow ignorance. To urge you to write a reply seems rather presumptuous from one whose knowledge of Marshall is what it probably is.

So much for M[arshall].

Later in the week I shall send you the tentative selections for the *Readings in Price Theory*. We put in your and Jimmie's article,[323] – which Boulding[324] has not yet read! I haven't canvassed many marginal and unknown items, but I'm inclined to push Abramovitz' oligopoly article.[325] Between the steel affair[326] (am I getting some dirty criticism!), these readings, our ph.d. qualifying exams, my bureau work, teaching, doctoral exams, the AER work (Homan[327] is in England), being external examiner at Swarthmore, and minor chores, I find it possible to keep occupied.

Jerry is improving, but still requires 2–3 months in bed. We're going to Canada nevertheless. Its some problem to keep him down.

Regards

George

I got your notes on costs today; at a very hasty skimming they look very good. I infer – this is my inferring day – that you're writing that treatise, willy nilly.

P.S.
   Who can I get on the rationing and income effects of rent control for FH?[328] Homer Jones failed me. Would Gale Johnson be available?[329]

November 15, 1950

Dear George:

I have been meaning to drop you a note for weeks & can offer only constitutional procrastination as explanation for not doing so.

We are now wonderfully ensconced in Paris, after spending the first 3 weeks in a hotel.[330] We now have a magnificent house, complete with maid & the use of a car for the rest of the period. The kids are going to a French school, & Rose to the Alliance Francaise to study French. I am struggling along with my pre-war French, just managing to keep afloat.

The trip over was excellent, & Paris is wonderful. We all like the French people & France. As an old & experienced traveler I needn't expatiate. The Americans here are being treated much, much too well. I mean those working for the gov't. Their real income is often on a level that would require an income of at least 20 to 25 thousand at home.

I have been most impressed, economically, by the enormous rigidity of the European economies. Stop talking about monopoly in USA at all. By comparison with Europe, we have the most perfect of perfect competition. The stories one hears are hair-raising. Even our steel & aluminum industrialists when they come over here are shocked at the restrictions they find.

Spent a week recently in Germany. It was terribly depressing on many levels. I have seldom had so strong an emotional reaction as I did when we first drove into Germany. All the hatred of years suddenly spilled out in a tremendous revulsion; every face I saw was a Nazi face – & people since have told me that maybe I was right. Rose felt the same way about – we both did so strongly that the first day we drove until 4 o'clock in the p.m. before eating lunch so we could get to an American army snack bar. This feeling got much moderated as we saw & talked with Germans & found them, of course, pleasant normal human beings. The destruction is really terrible & that part of it is depressing & arouses great sympathy.

Last Sunday we drove to Chartres, to see the cathedral. It is beautiful & enormously impressive. The economics of the cathedrals would be fascinating – has any body ever done any thing?

Accidentally ran into Robbins[331] in a restaurant the other day. He was over for one day only – probability? Sent his best to you. In our brief discussion of England he sounded terribly like an apologist for the labor government! Hope we can get over to England.

Arthur[332] arrives here tomorrow. He says he's had a wonderful time in England.

We return on the Liberté leaving here December 27. How are you all? – Jerry, in particular.

>Our love to you all,

>Milton

>January 5, 1951

Professor Milton Friedman
Department of Economics
University of Chicago
Chicago, Ill.

Dear Milt:

As you know, the American Economic Association is bringing out a volume of Readings in Price Theory this year, edited by Boulding and me.[333]

We request your permission to include in the volume your and Savage's[334] article, "The Utility Analysis of Choices Involving Risk," *Journal of Political Economy*, 1948, pp. 279–304.

If you will consent to its republication, we should also like to get a reprint and a list of any changes or additions you wish to make. And could we ask you to obtain Savage's permission?

>Cordially,

>George J. Stigler

January 15, 1950 [1951]

Dear George:

I feel like a heel for not having called you or seen you on our way through New York, but it was just a mad rush. We finally got off the pier about 11 o'clock, went straight out to Rahway [NJ] to see my mother,[335] from whence I proceeded shortly after two on to Chicago, while Rose and the kids took a train back to New York to get on a four o'clock plane to Chicago. The rush undoubtedly reflected an overevaluation of the desirability of our getting back to Chicago in time for me to meet classes on Thursday, but with our new 8 week quarter, we only meet classes 16 times a quarter, and I had already missed one meeting. In any event, it turned out well. I had mild if rainy weather driving across; immediately after my arrival it got cold and everything froze up, so I would have had more trouble driving. I should also apologize for being such a damn poor correspondent. But writing is such a poor substitute for talking. I expect however to see you soon – not later than March 30.

Europe was fine, except for one thing: I had to put in too many hours at the office for appearances sake. I can't say I did anything worth while. I wrote a bunch of memoranda to be neglected; saw a lot of people; found out quite a lot about Europe; found out how much I didn't and still don't know and how much a handicap it is not to be fluent in the language of the country you stay in. Europe is currently a mess, matched only by us. Nobody wants to fight, everybody is convinced that resistance is futile by Europe alone, nobody wants to be "liberated" (this is for the continent; England is a different story). There is an almost fatalistic acceptance of the idea of being occupied by the Russians. Some of the French who feel differently think all this would be changed suddenly and dramatically if Europe were really convinced that we would meet the initial onslaught alongside them and that we would put in enough to make an effective resistance somewhere in the middle of Germany fairly likely. As one Frenchman put it – put a million US and British soldiers on the continent of Europe and within two months there will be four million French with them. I'm somewhat dubious; the disintegration is I fear deeper than that. But nonetheless I'm inclined to think the risk is well worth taking – better to have lousy allies than none at all. This spring seems to me the critical time. Before leaving Europe I was inclined to say that there was one chance in four the Russians would attack in the spring; I'm now inclined to double the chances after seeing the degree of disunity and defeatism here. I have no doubt that ultimately we will move in the right direction so far as support for Europe is concerned; but that only makes the danger of attack in Europe this spring higher if we don't move rapidly and effectively between now and then to offer some barrier to Russian movement. The only hope is that the atomic bomb will be enough to deter them. God knows there is nothing else to do so if we don't really go to town in the next few months.

Politics aside, the things that most impressed us about Europe were the high inequality of income and the (related) terrific rigidity in the economic structure, the concept of free enterprise as freedom for everybody to protect his particular vested interest of the moment. By comparison, America is perfectly competitive – you don't need to measure the degree of monopoly; it's zero. Apparently the evil effects of the status economy and the rigidities were formerly much mitigated by international trade. The enormous extent of direct control over international trade now has the opposite effect. Our efforts to liberalize trade have had some success but on the whole a relatively minor one. An absolute precondition for their being more effective is I think a system of flexible exchange rates. If you or I were in charge of one of those economies and had to operate with rigid exchange rates under present day conditions I very much fear we would use direct controls over trade too. There was some sentiment for flexible exchange rates but not enough in high enough places.[336]

Germany was in the midst of a big boom when we were there. But it had an exchange crisis and met it by internal deflationary means rather than by exchange flexibility and I understand that since then the decline in unemployment has stopped and instead unemployment has been increasing rapidly. Nonetheless Germany will be back soon, given peace. Unfortunately or fortunately depending on your view, the Germans will and do work hard. England surprised me the most. It had the external appearance of real prosperity. How to explain it is a puzzle. But on all these, Arthur[337] has undoubtedly given you a far better report than I can.

In the realm of economic ideas, one of the most interesting phenomena – which may not be new to you and should not have been but was to me – is the fetish of investment. Investment has become the magic word to solve all problems just as gold or discount rate once was (or were? My English has gotten away from me). The most obvious manifestation is the enormous value attached to high aggregate investment. The rate of investment by European countries is terrific considering their level of living. But everybody seems to take it for granted that more and yet more is required, that defense expenditures, for example, must come at the expense of consumption, not of sacrosanct investment. More interesting is the extent to which investment is thought of as the cure to all specific ills. There is talk, say, of freeing trade in some commodity among a number of countries. This would mean that some country say would be under pressure to reduce its production of that commodity. The cure – invest enough in that industry in that country so it will be able to "compete" after trade is freed and won't have to contract. Of course this nonsense is possible only because of the related conception of loans as sums to be repaid only if it causes no hardship to the debtors. I could go on for a long time with such examples but you see the point.

We spent a couple of days at the London School which we enjoyed no end. It's a real interesting place. Robbins[338] wants to know if I would come over for part or all of next year if it could be arranged. Should I think of it seriously?

The kids I think got the most out of the trip. They went to a little French private school that we thought was wonderful, picked up an amazing amount of French, and enjoyed it thoroughly. We lived in a style that we have never equalled in the past and never shall again. If you want a high standard of living, join the foreign service.

Nothing much new here except for Hutchins' forthcoming departure.[339] Hope we have a substantial drop of students like you expect. So far however no such good luck.

Our very best to you all. Hope I can take your final sentence to mean that Jerry is fine and in normal circulation again. Rose awaits your communication with bated breath.

Yours,

[Milton]

January 15, 1951

Professor Milton Friedman
Department of Economics
University of Chicago
Chicago 37, Illinois

Dear Milton:

The Universities–National Bureau Committee for Economic Research plans to hold a conference on Business Concentration and Price Policy in the Spring of 1952.[340] The program of the conference is in the charge of a steering committee consisting of Corwin Edwards, Carl Kaysen, Edward Mason, Clair Wilcox and myself.

Could you be prevailed upon to give a paper on conceptual problems in the measurement of private and social economies of scale? This is a bewildered area of economic research, and I know you have done some thinking about it. You could choose those aspects of the problem that interested you. I shall not elaborate on all the advantages of doing this paper: systematising your ideas, stimulating research, influencing policy, adding a chapter to your treatise, etc. But I hope you will think of them.

Our plan is to have the papers mimeographed two months before the conference (that is, about February 1952), and circulated to all members of the conference. Hence only summaries or additional remarks will be presented orally, and the sessions will be devoted to discussion of the papers. The papers and discussion will be published. If you can accept this invitation, all the details of the conference will be sent to you as soon as possible. Where the institution with which a speaker is connected does not pay the costs of travel, the Universities-National Bureau Committee will do so.

Sincerely yours,

George J. Stigler

GJS:cd

January 19, 1951

Professor George J. Stigler
Faculty of Political Science
Columbia University
New York, 27, New York

Dear George:

Savage and I will be very glad to give you permission to include our article "The Utility Analysis of Choices Involving Risk," *Journal of Political Economy*, 1948, pages 279–304 in the forthcoming volume of *Readings in Price Theory*.

The only corrections that we would like to make before republication are on page 288 of the attached reprint.[341] I trust the insertion to indicate the corrections will be self explanatory.

Sincerely yours,

Milton Friedman

MF:rm

March 2, 1951

Professor George Stigler
Department of Political Science
Columbia University
New York City, New York

Dear George:

I don't believe I have ever answered your letter of January 15th asking whether I could prepare a paper of Economics of Scale. The answer you expect, of course, is the right one, "no." I have been wasting too much time doing nothing.

I have scanned through your article and like it very much, but I want to go through it more carefully before I turn it over to the JPA [JPE].[342]

My main reason for writing just now is that I am going on a week's junket in the East; the week of March 19th. I shall spend Monday, Tuesday, and Wednesday at Harvard and part of Friday afternoon and evening at Princeton. I plan to come down to New York sometime Thursday morning and leave there sometime on Friday afternoon. You and Arthur[343] are, of course, the two people I most want to see, and I am hoping that some how we can plan to spend the evening together.

I am writing to Arthur now.

Our very best to the family.

Sincerely,

Milton Friedman

MF/s

Tuesday [June, 1951]

Dear Milton

As we have both feared, I have decided to decline the Chicago offer. I must say that I have not found this an easy decision, and I have no deep conviction that it has been a wise one.

Financially – I almost said economically – there is a large sacrifice in leaving. Columbia raised me to $10,000 after you called, and with the NB[344] the total is $14,000. Hence the move would cost almost $3000 a year, if I make an allowance for moving costs. This seems a large cost.

On the professional side, it may be that the balance is ambiguous. There is no one whose advice and company I value more than yours, but there are few other great attractions in the present Chicago economics department. I'm not the least bit inclined to boast of Columbia, which has a fine assortment of damn fools, but the N.B. crowd – if one may average a universe ranging from Arthur to Mills[345] – has a lot of sense and knowledge. Arthur has perhaps too strong a desire to formulate a program of research – the thing which, if successful, is called an architectonic sense – but I wouldn't want to go beyond this. And if I can formulate a really significant study, I'm confident he'll further it.

This decision is most unhappy in that it disappoints good friends and does not elate me. It seems fundamentally improper for us to be at different schools and I don't like to continue the impropriety. But so be it.

George

Our address is almost immediately to be
Windermere
Ontario
Canada

July 14 [1951]

Dear Milt

As I wrote before, I asked Schultz for a postponement until this fall, partly no doubt out of uncertainty, partly because I shudder at the thought of moving by the time the boys must go to school.[346] He has not replied. I don't understand Arthur's[347] museum piece allegory – I'm not as valuable, or endearing, or prospectively indolent, as the phrase sounds to me. Anyway, I am now trying to think out my future, but finding it less engrossing than admiring Jerry swim.

I have read your note[348] and I like it very much. My only question of form is whether you don't overwork the connection with the "real" income demand curve, granting that there is a little connection. If this is so, then the note must stand on its own feet, and not be simply an annex to the Marshallian one.[349] And then the only question is whether it is worth <u>your</u> while to publish it, granting that it is more clever and sensible than what others have published. I can't see any good reason for not publishing it, or any very strong reason for publishing. That's helpful, isn't it?

I hope to get down to work, after working through the intolerable silliness of Malthus' population and his political economy. I've drafted a series of articles on the Ricardian system[350] and will in the fall round them out and send them to you.

Regards

George

5731 Kenwood Ave.
Chgo 37, Ill.

[winter or spring 1952]

Dear George:

I see by the enclosed clipping that you shall be here Friday – I knew of course that you were coming sometime but had forgotten or never knew the exact date. Are you staying over? If so, how about having dinner with us? We are having some other people over for dinner that night, including the Hayeks,[351] Schultz's,[352] & Leo Szilard (the most entertaining of this lot) & we would be more than delighted to have you join us. If you do, you might as well stay overnight here. We can readily put you up, as you know.

At long last, I have gotten around to reading your paper (on Riccy)[353] with some care. I am, as you well know, incompetent to judge it, so I enjoyed it very much indeed. I had two rather general comments, but one is rendered obsolete by your note to Earl,[354] which he showed to me. I thought the first two sections did, & the third did not, live up to the promise of the first page – "a reappraisal of his system." My other general comment is re Malthus' theory of population.[355] Your castigation of him may be fully justified for all I know, but is your implication that his theory is thoroughly discredited? We have talked before of reinterpreting its guts to mean that children are to be treated like commodities on which income is expended; that the number of children "purchased" will be a function of their relative cost, compared to other commodities, cost of course including as a negative cost the expected return from them. Your calculations of cost of purchasing children in city & country are a highly plausible explanation of the differential birth rates. The farming community produces not only agricultural products but also laborers, & it ships its "excess" production of the one and of the other to the city. In this sense it seems to me less than correct to say "he gave little guidance to later economists on how to construct a theory." The difficulty was that importance was attached to the idea of a number ("subsistence") instead of to a functional relation; but this was a rather common failing of the classical school, I take it.

Most of my other comments are utterly trivial. But I might mention a number just to show that my failure to list more is not because I didn't read your paper carefully.

On p. 4 of the part on rent in a footnote you write, "Third, he argued that wages & profits are both high in America, so high wages are not the cause of low profits. But at most this shows they are not the only cause."

The logic of this escapes me completely. Let high wages be the <u>only</u> cause of low profits; let the presence of Indians be the <u>only</u> cause of high profits; let the latter be stronger than the former. I take it the copulation is the only cause of children; is this disproved by the existence of a childless, yet ardent, couple? What it seems is that they are not a <u>sufficient</u> cause, while West[356] wanted to show it to be no cause at all.

In your criticism of Ricardo you come close to "the assumptions aren't true, hence the theory isn't true" position. Of course, his assumptions were foolish; so shall it always be; where is the evidence that they produced seriously invalid results? This is one of the respects in which I was most dubious about this section. You tell us something about the innards of the clock – to take your analogy – but little about what time it told & whether it told the right time. And was Ricardo really so wrong here?

Do you want your draft back? If so, I'll give it to you when you are here.

Yours,

Milton Friedman

Cost of Raising a Boy
on a North Central Farm, 1935–36
(Family Income: $2000–3000)

Age	Food	Clothing	Medical Care	Self-Supporting	Interest (at 3%)	Total
Birth						$300
0–1	$42	$10	$12		$10	374
1–2	42	10	10		12	448
2–3	45	20	9		15	537
3–4	45	20	12		17	631
4–5	51	20	15		20	737
5–6	51	26	15		23	852
6–7	51	26	13		27	969
7–8	66	26	9		31	1101
8–9	66	26	8		35	1236
9–10	74	26	8		39	1383
10–11	74	26	8		43	1534
11–12	79	33	8		48	1702
12–13	79	33	9		53	1876
13–14	88	33	9		58	2064
14–15	88	33	9	−$17	64	2241
15–16	88	52	10	−33	69	2427
16–17	89	52	10	−55	74	2597
17–18	89	52	11	−77	79	2751

Food: Average food purchased per person in 2-person families is $87.50
Rent: No increase in number of rooms
Clothing: Consumer purchases study
Medical Care: Average expenditures per person in 2-person families is $14.
Self-Supporting: In 1940 the percentages of farm male children in labor force were:

    age 15, 13.1 percent
    age 16, 22.3 percent
    age 17, 36.2 percent
    age 18, 50.4 percent

Cost of Raising a Boy
in New York and Chicago, 1935–36
(Family Income: $2000–3000)

Age	Food	Clothing	Medical Care	Rent	Self-Supporting	Interest (at 3%)	Total
Birth							$300
0–1	$156	$16	$42	75		$13	602
1–2	156	16	36	75		22	907
2–3	166	24	32	75		32	1236
3–4	166	24	44	75		42	1587
4–5	188	24	52	75		53	1979
5–6	188	34	52	75		65	2393
6–7	188	34	45	75		77	2812
7–8	247	34	31	75		90	3289
8–9	247	34	29	75		104	3778
9–10	273	34	28	75		119	4307
10–11	273	34	29	75		135	4853
11–12	292	43	30	75		152	5445
12–13	292	43	30	75		170	6055
13–14	325	43	32	75		189	6719
14–15	325	43	33	75	−$10	209	7394
15–16	325	56	34	75	−23	229	8090
16–17	332	56	37	75	−70	249	8769
17–18	332	56	40	75	−149	268	9391

Food: Average food expenditure per person in 2-person families ($325) multiplied by equivalent-adult fractions (Dublin and Lotka, *The Money Value of a Man*, p. 50[357])

Clothing: Average expenditures reported in Consumer Purchases Study[358]

Medical Care: Average medical expenditures per person in 2-person families ($50) multiplied by equivalent adult fractions (ibid.)

Rent: Rent and household operation costs per room ($125) times .6. Families with 1 child have about .6 more rooms than those with none.

Self-supporting: In 1940 the percentages of urban children in the labor force were:

    age 15, 2.2 percent

    age 16, 4.6 percent

    age 17, 14.1 percent

    age 18, 29.7 percent

November 30 [1952]

Dear Milt

I'm inclined to go along with you on the use of a theory, but what do you think of the following reformulation:

1. After a theory has been developed and tested and much used, its applicability to certain classes of problems becomes established. These classes of problems may be completely specific or objective, as in the use of engineering formulas. Or they may be more loosely specified.
2. At all times there will also be many questions that do not clearly fall within or without the domain of the theory, and only further experiment can tell us whether a given problem should be handled by a given theory.

This distinction is partly inaccurate, in that even under 1 the theory will be less than perfectly precise, and it is also trivial, in that it says only that some things are known better than others. But still it helps me to reconcile our views. You are clearly thinking of class 2 most of the time; whereas I put more weight on class 1. The routine work of a science falls mostly in 1; the improvements of a science in 2.

Most of your revised pp. 26ff seem ok to me, but I have 2 questions.[359]

1. Why do you call only profit maximizing an assumption? Surely all the other conditions have a right to be called assumptions too, – all but the one reserved as an implication.
2. Your shift to evidence of intent to monopolize is unfortunate. This is a legal concept, and it has wholly different significance than the word in theory (to some men, at least); hence we do not have a right to argue reinforcing support. It might be better to shift to an example involving only economic analysis.

No news here. I'm wasting all my time on committees of one sort or another, and reading Ricardo (the correspondence is fascinating).[360] Soon I think I'll spend some time thinking up ways [to] keep off the committee on appointment procedures, the committee on instruction, the social science research council, the committee to study a graduate student's proposed revision of the departmental courses (truly), etc.

[George]

15 Latham Road, Cambridge.
May 25, 1954

Dear George:

I have been meaning to write to you for literally months, and have no excuse other than sheer indolence for not doing so. This junketing life saps one's drives.[361]

Gather you have been having a high time with your celebrations at Columbia,[362] what currently with Robbins, Robertson, Lewis, and Roepke to keep you company.[363] What in the world induced you to give the third gentlemen mentioned an honorary degree? Or for that matter, the fourth? The program, which I recently had forwarded to me from Chicago looks fine on paper; one sheet that is, I can imagine what happened to it when it got on 3,436 sheets.

As you know, since I last wrote, we have been in Spain for a week (just Rose and I, we left the kids here); and all of us in Sweden and Denmark for three weeks. We go next week to Wales for a few days, come back here for two weeks, then up to Scotland for two weeks, then to France for 10 days, then sail July 15. Nice life, eh! (But don't ask me what work I haven't done!)

Spain was extraordinarily interesting and I strongly recommend it to you. In the first place, Spanish hospitality has to be experienced to be believed. We were foiled in buying the things we wanted to in Toledo because some of the Spanish professors took us there and if we so much as touched something, they immediately proceeded to buy it for us. Part of it is of course mannerism, but I believe part also reflects the feeling of being closed in, or rather of having been so, and an enormous desire to make contact with outsiders. No pictures of Franco, except on the money. Utterly free casual conversation, including warning that you must not be misled by it, that nothing beyond speech – private speech, that is, – is free. University library contains all periodicals, including *New Statesman* and *Nation*. Social policy on surface is that of welfare state, including extensive social security program, prohibition on firms of firing people, gov't investment and nationalization programs, forn exchge [foreign exchange] control, etc. Perhaps what surprised me the most was to find most of the younger people Keynesians and planners in the British sense. The great inequality between rich and poor, poverty of poor, etc., was as expected. You don't see it much in Madrid, but you sure do in the countryside. Madrid is a lovely town and the Prado clearly the most exciting museum we have been in. It is really a wonderful country for tourists even if not for its inhabitants so you must put it on your itinerary for next year.

Sweden and Denmark are of course altogether different. Much less divergent from your own experience – indeed, Sweden is amazingly like the U.S. – and partly therefore much more pleasant but not so stimulating. When we first drove into the country in Sweden – above Gothenberg where we landed – David[364] said, "This smells like New Hampshire," and it certainly does. Same kind of rolling country with many rivers and lakes – because created by same kind of glacial era. Same kind of trees – spruces, pines, firs, birch, etc. In most of Europe, houses are built of brick or stone; in Sweden like much of the US, houses in the countryside are built of wood and for the same obvious reason. In most of Europe (not England of course) you have the strip farming system, so little villages are scattered through the countryside with open fields in between. In Sweden like US have individual farms. Etc. The result is that if you were dropped in either NH or Sweden without knowing which, you might very well have difficulty knowing which. In addition the people, the stores, etc., all strike you as like the US. Here again a common cause. The industrial revolution came late in both countries and about the same time and both countries have been spared the physical ravages of war since. There is less appearance of extreme poverty than at home; more uniformity at the bottom and greater homogeneity of population; but not clearly any less inequality above the bottom. Sweden struck me as much less of a socialist country than I had supposed – and than England. The economists, I should add, are active, interesting, and able. I haven't had any better, if as good, professional talk anywhere. The person who impressed me the most is Erik Lundberg who is a wonderful person. All in all, as you can see, we liked Sweden immensely. Our one regret – particularly Rose's, though I don't disagree, is that she didn't bludgeon me into spending enough time and money to buy a mess of furniture, which is beautiful and so cheap it would pay to send it. Denmark is a lovely country to tour through but not so interesting in other ways.

Only enough room to ask your plans. Best to all of you from all of us.

Milton

P.S. Kids & Rose all well. David is being a cricket enthusiast & threatens to introduce game in U.S. Janet starting to put on English accent – but will knock that out quickly. Rose put on Swedish weight on smorgasbord etc, but is knocking that off quickly. Trust you're all well.

October 19 [1954]

Dear Milt

Your letter reveals that we view the NB[365] differently, and that your view is more favorable than mine! (I realize how readily this can be turned.) The directors of research, Arthur more than Sol,[366] have largely considered their task to be how to staff projects for which they have funds, not how to finance the staff. I base this not only upon my own history, but also upon such events as the falling out of Arthur and Kuznets[367] (who would not shift his interests), and the persuasion of such experts as Gold-smith, Mack, and Nutter[368] to work on the Russian study.

Sol is less forceful and overwhelming than Arthur, and he had broached work in industrial organization some time ago. Still a talk would only lead to agreements in principle and leave all in the air. I am now preparing a project in the area for submission to Ford.[369] It will be acted upon in February. If it is not accepted, with or without Ford money, in the spring, while I am in Europe, I believe the issue will be permanently settled.

To return to your letter, I do not think it probable that at present I would accept a generous offer – as the last one was – at present.

Nor do I think that you should delay a decision when the rewards of delay are estimated so low. (Quite aside from myself, however, I see no reason why Chicago should make any hasty decisions in any area – a year or two is nothing in the life of a famous department of economics.)

Whether it is necessary or not, I should like to add that these latter paragraphs are not easy to write: there is no one anywhere I would rather have as a colleague than you, and no one soon at Chicago who I would not enjoy as a colleague. Since I cannot say as much of Columbia, I should be logical in my conclusions and actions. If I am not, it is because I am loathe to uproot a family for less than major professional preferences. It is not reassuring to me that the writing of this letter leaves me less confident I am acting properly than I was when I started!

As ever

George

Oct 25 [1954]

Dear Milt

The enclosed comments are for your edification.[370]

In looking them over, my references to wealth now seem a little obscure. What I have in mind fundamentally is a more explicit transition from the formal theory to the specific hypothesis, – attention to wealth as income, as reserve (Pigou effect) etc.

Regards

George

Friedman's Monograph

I shall skip the praises this splendid piece deserves. I shall not even press the obvious recommendation: why not make all the tests of the hypothesis that are proposed, so that this would become a definitive treatment, not an extra-ordinarily suggestive essay. The following suggestions are essentially minor.

p. 12	It could be argued that it is a tacit assumption in the literature that income is constant through time. A few words might be devoted to (1) effects of the assumption, and (2) its untenable nature.
p. 17	This crucial step deserves some further elaboration, or perhaps even less. The present argument could be used to say that the ratio of pounds of sowbelly consumed to pounds of steak consumed is independent of their absolute prices, given money income. Instead of an equal ignorance assumption, I would prefer good old Occam's razor.
p. 20	It appears that the uncertainty calls for a new technique, but is this fundamental?
	Bottom: Shouldn't increased wealth allow increased diversification and reduce risks?
p. 22, note 2:	Perhaps I am mistakenly worried by the repeated use of the "pure number" argument. The ratio of the strength of a man to that of a woman is a pure number; why should it depend in any obvious way on how much they (equally) eat? Yet it may be reversed at certain caloric levels.
p. 24	If Swedes and Mexicans differ in response to given circumstances, does u embrace this? That is, is this variable u such that all units have the same function?

p. 25	Is it reasonable to assume that income and tastes are uncorrelated?
p. 36	"entirely implausible" is trick writing.
p. 38	If the technique is applicable to wealth, somewhere you should remark on it. In any event, the neglect of all other variables in your consumption function should be explained somewhere along the line.
p. 45	Would not a brief appendix, essentially reproducing the relevant sections of Income from Independent Professional Practice be desirable?
p. 49	Doesn't "existing evidence" mean existing empirical generalizations?
p. 57	bottom, 1931? 1939? In general here you press the details so hard that it creates suspicion rather than confidence in the hypothesis. The theory isn't supposed to be right every year, – the data aren't that good.
p. 65	Here the permanent component seems implicitly to be defined for an unusually long time period. Shouldn't wealth be mentioned here too?
p. 87	It is somewhat confusing to take Tobin's evidence against the relative income status, examine it, and then on occasion bring it to bear on your more sophisticated version. Why not skip the relative status and indicate the relevance of his evidence for your theory, and separately or anyway incidentally discuss its relevance to the relative status theory.
p. 122	Date this comparison.
p. 129	Is not the opening sentence too strong?

Should a "saving clause" be used? That is, segregate your contributions re (1) $C = KY$, (2) decomposition of observations. Also note that latter does not have to be used only with consumption functions linear in the observed variables, or with zero mean transitory components, etc. – and perhaps more general cases will not be found to be mathematically or statistically unworkable.

Tuesday [November or
December 1954]

Dear Milt

At the moment only 1 name occurs to me, and unfortunately I do not know him too well. He is Leland Yeager, a Ph.D. of 2 years ago, now an assistant professor at Maryland.

He has published – a year ago in the AER – a denunciation of Domar,[371] but would be better judged by his thesis, a many-sided defense of free exchange rates.[372] You see he has good prejudices. He is a young man of considerable intellectual power and has an independent and critical mind. He is personally shy, and may be a poor teacher.

The enclosure is designed, not to prove I am busy (it is an old piece) but because it may interest you.[373] I hope to make a better empirical application in the reasonable future.

Regards

George

P.S.
     Since neither one of us is going to Detroit,[374] I hope to see you in NY!

May 14 [1955]

Dear Milt

I have just been to Zurich,[375] and Hunold[376] was – as usual – very cordial and the soul of kindness in doing favors. The trip stimulates me to express an idea, which I had already had – why don't you get Van Sickle[377] to invite Hunold to the US for that meeting this fall?

I think the invitation could be defended simply for all the work Hunold has done for the Mont Pelerin group, but that is not why I write. Hunold sounds financially strapped, and is looking hard for some additional income. He could use the trip to the US to approach some foundations [PAGE TORN] institute, and that is why I have [PAGE TORN] . . . tter.

It is hard to believe that so much of our visit is over. In 5 weeks we leave Geneva for a month in Germany, and then we begin to drift homeward.

I've been reading a fair amount of Swiss economic literature and I am impressed by how much of the error of their ways – or so I see it – is due to very poor economic analysis. The cartel literature is very sad, and Friedrich Lutz tells me no one would listen to his pleas (especially in Germany) for flexible foreign exchange rates.

Vous avez tort – j'ai appris la langue française très, très bien. Mais les garçons, non, non.

George

30 Avenue Jacques Martin
Geneve

May 6, 1955

Dear Van Sickle:

In principle I should like to attend the meeting that you are arranging for October 13–16. Unfortunately, however, I have left not only my duties, but also my records of future duties, in New York, and not until I return in August will I know for certain whether I can attend the meeting. If this proviso is acceptable, I should be glad to make a tentative acceptance.

You might consider whether the issues raised by "competition" are not essentially technical, so that a more controversial question, like the role of the state in directing individual economic behavior, would perhaps be a better springboard for discussion.

Sincerely

George J. Stigler

Dear Milton –
Do you & the others care to make any comment on Stigler's suggestion? No one has refused our invitation to date.
J[ohn]V[an]S[ickle]

[Jan or Feb 1956]

Dear Milt

You might take a look at this if you are due for some lectures on competition,[378] – or pass it on to Aaron[379] if you're busy. The smaller thing was my comment at the Christmas meetings.[380]

Will I see you in Phil[adelphia], Feb 27–8?

George

December 5, 1956

Dear George:

Every time I get a letter from you, on no matter what, I find myself making the same remark after reading it, namely, "George is wonderful," and the letter just received on Arthur[381] is no exception.

I saw Arthur at length a week ago Sunday just before he made his final decision & I am sure as a result that your interpretation is entirely correct. I put it differently– that he has been the "boss" of a large enterprise for the past 10 years & likes it, provided it is the right enterprise – but I think your way of putting it is better.

The Bureau deserves congratulations for its imagination in rearranging things so as to enable Arthur to come in at the top without displacing anyone. I remain persuaded that if they had not worked out such an arrangement, the result would have been the opposite. I find it hard to see anything more we could have done and, if we made any mistake, it was, I fear, to do too much. After my talk with Arthur, I am also convinced that he did the right thing in terms of his values – in the more than trivial sense that he will not regret it. What I am less sure about is whether the arrangement will lead to his making as important a contribution to economics as he would if he came here – but that is to impose a different set of values.

We too have accepted the invitation to Ford Heaven[382] & are delighted that we shall have you as neighbors. How's your tennis? I hope it has degenerated enough so that I will be a passable opponent. I understand, too, that skiing is not inconvenient. We are acquiring skis & going for a few days up to Michigan before X-mas. I take it you, like I, remain firm in your decision not to go to the meetings this year.[383]

I enjoyed greatly both the pieces you sent me – the one on Rogin (where is it for?)[384] and the one on survival as a test of optimum size.[385] I read through the latter once & liked it very much, then put it aside to read it through carefully a second time so that I could send some sensible comments. That is where it is now & that is still my plan.

Barger[386] has asked me to participate in a panel in N.Y. on Jan 17 on Federal aid to universities & I have agreed to do so. I did so partly because I could combine it with a talk to your grad econ club, who have invited me several times in the past couple of years & whom I have always turned down. Unless you veto the suggestion, I plan to talk to them on "The Income–Expenditure Theory & the Qu Th of Mon, an Empirical Comparison"[387] and to present some of our empirical results comparing the predictive accuracy of the two. This seems to me better than the consumption function, which should be in print in a few months,[388] or than my current work on money, which I am not yet ready to generalize from in any broad way.

Having failed on Stigler & Burns, & being a believer in judging hypotheses by their conformity to experience, I am not sure I can accept your characterizations of Chicago & Columbia. The proof of the pudding seems to be in the beating we have gotten. More important, where should we turn next? Or should we be content with our stable of youngsters & with adding to them?

Our best to the family – I greatly enjoyed my last visit with you all & look forward to more of the same.

Yours,

Milton

May 15, 1957

Dear George:

I like your piece on local gov't[389] very much, though I think I have some differences with you on it. I have been refraining from returning it to you until I could go over it again, which I intend to do very shortly, & send you more detailed comments.

I write now on a different, more immediate, & more practical matter. A month or more ago I wrote Allen[390] asking whether any problem was raised at the Center[391] by the Bureau[392] stipend. Not hearing from him for so long, I assumed the answer was no & so sent off my blank to Tyler[393] re financial arrangements a couple of days ago without saying anything about it. Today, I got a letter from Allen in which he says "I think you ought to present the facts on that to Ralph Tyler fully, & ask his decision" & suggests that he thinks it will raise a real problem.

Before checking with Tyler definitely, I thought I would ask you – since you are doubtless in the same position as I am – what if anything you have done about it. Have you said anything to Ralph?

My feeling was that it was better not to raise the issue if it seemed reasonably clear what the situation was, & I assumed that since the NBER business interfered in no way with my activity at Palo Alto that it would be irrelevant. However, Allen's comment puts it into a somewhat different light, which is why I write you.

My memory is terrible & I do not recall at all whether we ever talked about this.

I shall appreciate a quick answer since if something should be done, it should be done quickly.

Best regards to all.

Yours,

Milton

May 22, 1957

Dear George:

Your arguments, both verbal and written are persuasive. They have convinced me (with a nudge from Rose) to disregard Allen's[394] comments & do nothing further about it, except to write him & tell him (a) that this is my conclusion & (b) briefly why. I shall not, of course, bring your name into my correspondence with WA[llen]W[allis].

Rose asked me especially to tell you how much she enjoyed your postscript, especially the crack about a "part time dean."

I enclose also, for your interest, a carbon copy of my letter re the tax matter, for your amusement.

Thanks much for helping me to make up my mind. At least, if any problems arise, we will have one another for comfort. My apologies, too, for ever having raised the matter with WAW in the first place.

Yours,

Milton

May 25, 1957

Dear George:

I have just been rereading your local govt piece[395] which I return here-
with, and I am much puzzled by some aspects of it – which partly shows
what a thought-provoking and fine piece it is.

My first puzzle is re the emphasis on redistribution. If the argument
here is right, surely you do not carry it far enough. Why not redistribute
directly to individuals and let them use their incomes to buy the governmental services that they want and so get the private enterprise provision
of governmental services that is suggested by equal real incomes except
for the "excessive freedom" it allows to individuals? Is it only because of
the problem of monopoly and excessive freedom? I must confess that I
find it hard to say yes; on the other hand, I cannot construct any other
explanation. Again, the answer will be made that grants of funds carry
with it control, but your answer to that objection in re[gard] to grants to
local communities applies equally here.

My second puzzle is the other side of this: can the external economy
argument be dismissed as readily as you in effect dismiss it? Take education. It is argued (by you and me) that there is justification for compulsory
education because by educating our children we benefit others. This
requires on this level and without distributive considerations no public
school system or financial aid but only the imposition and enforcement of
compulsory minimum education. Could this be done via voluntary and
private communities? Community A has as part of its contract for anybody
to live in it and affecting the amount he pays that only those enter here
who have had a certain minimum of education and who agree to give their
children the corresponding minimum. This doesn't quite seem satisfactory,
but maybe the only reason is one of scale: we want some element of
community on a national scale to prevent fragmentation into separate city-
states.

What I suppose bothers me about the universalizing of private corpora-
tions on a general scale – incidentally a clever way of posing the issue – is
this point on a broader level. Rule out all problems of redistribution and of
"excessive freedom." It seems to me we still need some public "forum" or
"marketplace" with access by all in which to make our deals whether of
legislation or private contract, in which to make the rules of the game and
to play it. Or am I wrong in this? If all communities and equally all roads,
etc. were private, would my interest in being able to make the best contract lead me to provide sufficient access? As I ask it, I don't really see
why not.

I guess what this comes down to is that it is only external effects that account for govt aside from redistribution and exc[essive] freedom and it is hard for us to distinguish between true "external effects" and other personal relationships. $2^{nd.}$, the problem of "monopoly" is more far-reaching than it seems because in order to have a large enough unit to encompass all significant external effects, you are driven to a scale which raises problems of "monopoly."

All of this is very confused & thereby properly reflects the state of my own mind.

Yours,

Milton

December 18, 1957

Agreement

We, the undersigned, have today entered a joint venture to purchase $40,000 in US Government Bonds (1970's), in the name and account of Milton Friedman. At the settlement of this venture, we agree to divide any costs, profits, or losses equally between ourselves.

George J. Stigler

Milton Friedman

Notes

Introduction

1 Stigler was Charles R. Walgreen Distinguished Service Professor of American Institutions in the Graduate School of Business from 1958 until his retirement in 1981. Friedman joined the faculty of the Department of Economics in 1946, was named Paul Snowdon Russell Distinguished Service Professor in 1962. Friedman retired from the faculty in 1977.

2 H. Laurence Miller, Jr., "On the 'Chicago School of Economics'," *Journal of Political Economy* 70 (February 1962): 64–9.

3 George J. Stigler, "On the 'Chicago School of Economics': Comment," *Journal of Political Economy* 70 (February 1962): 70–1.

4 The SRG was a unit of the National Defense Research Council. See W. Allen Wallis, "The Statistical Research Group, 1942–1945," *Journal of the American Statistical Association* 70 (June 1980): 320–30.

5 *Roofs or Ceilings? The Current Housing Problem.* Irvington-on-Hudson, NY: Foundation for Economic Education, 1946.

6 See G. S. Becker, "George Joseph Stigler: January 17, 1911–December 1, 1991," *Journal of Political Economy* 101 (October 1993): 762.

7 Stigler, *The Theory of Price*, New York: Macmillan, 1946; Friedman, *Price Theory: A Provisional Text*, Chicago: Aldine, 1962.

8 London: Macmillan, 1st edition, 1890, 8th edition, 1920.

9 Between June and November 1946 Friedman and Stigler exchanged nine letters about *Roofs or Ceilings*. Many of these letters had to do with a dispute with V. Orval Watts and Leonard E. Read, Editorial Director and President of the Foundation for Economic Education. Watts and Read feared that Friedman and Stigler's stated preference in the essay for more equality of income and wealth could be interpreted as a pro-collectivist statement.

10 Hart was a 1936 University of Chicago Ph.D.

11 Frank H. Knight.

12 Lloyd Mints.

13 H. Gregg Lewis.

14 Friedman did graduate work at both Chicago and Columbia, but took his Ph.D. from Columbia.

15 The reference was to financial support from the Ford Foundation.

16 The offer from Chicago was made on October 18, 1957. After a counter offer from Columbia, Stigler accepted Chicago's offer on November 30, 1957.

17   8th edition, London: Macmillan, 1920.
18   New York: Macmillan, 1946.
19   By summer 1946 the 8th edition of Marshall's *Principles* (1920) had been reprinted in 1922, 1925, 1927, 1930, 1936, 1938, and 1946. The reprint used by Friedman is unknown.
20   "The History of the Giffen Paradox: Notes" was published in the *Journal of Political Economy* 55 (April 1947), 152–6.
21   Chicago, IL: Aldine, 1962.
22   New York: Macmillan, 1942.
23   *American Economic Review* 37 (June 1947): 414–18.
24   *Five Lectures on Economic Problems*, London, New York: Longmans Green, 1949.
25   *Journal of Farm Economics* 23 (February 1941): 389–90. Triffin, Cambridge, MA: Harvard University Press, 1941.
26   "The Methodology of Positive Economics." In *Essays in Positive Economics*, pp. 3–43. Chicago, IL: University of Chicago Press, 1953; "The Marshallian Demand Curve." *Journal of Political Economy* 57 (December 1949): 463–95. The first draft of "The Methodology of Positive Economics" was titled "Descriptive Validity vs. Analytical Relevance in Economic Theory." Friedman completed it in the summer of 1948.
27   With basing point pricing the price of the product delivered to the customer is the base price plus the delivery cost from a fixed "basing point," regardless of where the seller is located.
28   "The Case for Flexible Exchange Rates." In *Essays in Positive Economics*, pp. 157–203. Chicago, IL: University of Chicago Press, 1953.
29   "The Development of Utility Theory." (2 pts) *Journal of Political Economy* 58 (August 1950): 307–27 and (October 1950): 373–96; "The Ricardian Theory of Value and Distribution." *Journal of Political Economy* 60 (June 1952): 187–207; "The Tenable Range of Functions of Local Government." In *Federal Expenditure Policies for Economic Growth and Stability*. 85th Congress, 1st session Joint Economic Committee. November 5, 1957.

Letters

1   Friedman wrote this letter while with the Statistical Research Group (SRG) based at Columbia University. The SRG was a component of the Office of Scientific Research and Development which organized scientific research for the U.S. government during World War II. Stigler had recently left the SRG and returned to the University of Minnesota where he was trying to help Friedman get an appointment. Friedman received an appointment and taught at Minnesota during the 1945–46 academic year.
2   Richard L. Kozelka, 1899–1985, was Acting Dean of the School of Business Administration, University of Minnesota, in 1944–45. He became Dean in 1945.
3   The work was published as H. A. Freeman, M. A. Girschik, and W. A. Wallis, (eds) Statistical Research Group, *Sequential Analysis of Statistical Data: Applications*, New York: Columbia University Press, 1945.
4   Friedman's contribution (Part IV, "Construction of Sampling Tables and Standard Procedure") in H. A. Freeman, M. Friedman, F. Mosteller, and W. A. Wallis, (eds) *Sampling Inspection: Principles, Procedures, and Tables for*

Single, Double, and Sequential Sampling in Acceptance Inspection and Quality Control Based on Percent Defective, New York and London: McGraw Hill, 1948, was based on the manual he prepared for the Navy.

5 Operating Characteristic (OC) curves refer to the probability, for a given sampling plan, of accepting an inspection lot as a function of the lot's quality level.

6 Fry was Acting Chief, Applied Mathematics Panel, National Defense Research Committee. The issue was whether to publish sequential analysis applications commercially. Fry was opposed to publication. The book was published; see footnote 3 and W. A. Wallis, "The Statistical Research Group, 1942–1945 (with discussion)."*Journal of the American Statistical Association* 1980, vol. 75, 320–33.

7 Milton and Rose Director Friedman's children were Janet, born February 26, 1943 and David, born February 12, 1945. At the time of this letter George and Margaret "Chick" Mack Stigler had two sons, Stephen, born August 10, 1941 and David, born August 31, 1943.

8 Lloyd Mints. The enclosure is missing.

9 The allusion is to the death of the University of Chicago Law Professor Henry C. Simons, June 19, 1946.

10 Leonard E. Read, President of the Foundation for Economic Education. The Foundation for Economic Education had agreed to publish a paper on rent ceilings that Friedman and Stigler co-wrote while teaching at the University of Minnesota. The paper was ultimately published in two versions: *Roofs or Ceilings? The Current Housing Problem*, Irvington-on-Hudson, NY: Foundation for Economic Education, 1946, and a condensed version with the same title distributed by the National Association of Real Estate Boards in 1946.

11 The Friedmans spent the first part of the summer of 1946 in Portland, Oregon, where Rose Friedman's family lived, and the latter part of the summer in Cannon Beach, Oregon.

12 The manuscript for *Roofs or Ceilings? The Current Housing Problem*.

13 In Providence, RI where Stigler had accepted a position at Brown University.

14 Indiana, PA where Margaret Stigler's family lived.

15 V. Orval Watts.

16 Leonard E. Read.

17 An early draft of the manuscript contains the following sentence: "For those, like us, who would like even more equality, not only for housing but for all products, it is surely better to attack directly existing inequalities in income and wealth than to ration each of the hundreds of commodities and services that compose our standard of living." Friedman and Stigler, "The Current Housing Problem: Ceilings or Roofs?" Manuscript, George J. Stigler Papers, Regenstein Library, University of Chicago. The phrase "like us" became a point of contention between Stigler and Friedman and the Foundation for Economic Education. The published manuscript retains the phrase but also includes an editor's footnote written by V. Orval Watts: "The authors fail to state whether the 'long-term measures' which they would adopt go beyond elimination of special privilege, such as monopoly now protected by government. In any case, however, the significance of their argument at this point deserves special notice. It means that, even from the standpoint of those who put equality above justice and liberty, rent controls are the 'height of folly'." *Roofs or Ceilings? The Current Housing Problem*, Irvington-on-Hudson, NY: Foundation for Economic Education, 1946, p. 10.

18 The deleted sentence was "Further, the personal income tax, which is admirably suited to reduce the inequality of income, is by the same token suited to take a considerable share of the incomes of prosperous landlords." Friedman and Stigler, "The Current Housing Problem: Ceilings or Roofs?" Manuscript, George J. Stigler Papers, Regenstein Library, University of Chicago.

19 Friedman sent a telegram to Read on August 9, 1946, and wrote a letter to confirm the telegram on August 10. See Addendum One.

20 Friedman was referring to draft of the manuscript of *Roofs or Ceilings? The Current Housing Problem*, which included editorial revisions suggested by V. Orval Watts, the editorial director of the Foundation for Economic Education.

21 *The Theory of Price*, New York: Macmillan, 1946.

22 Alfred Marshall, *Principles of Economics*, 8th edition, London: Macmillan, 1920.

23 By summer 1946 the eighth edition of Marshall's *Principles* (1920) had been reprinted in 1922, 1925, 1927, 1930, 1936, 1938 and 1946. The reprint used by Friedman is unknown.

24 "additionally" in the original.

25 V. Orval Watts.

26 *Roofs or Ceilings? The Current Housing Problem*.

27 Alfred Marshall.

28 Arthur F. Burns.

29 *The Theory of Price*. Stigler and Friedman shared an office at the University of Minnesota during the 1945–46 academic year.

30 V. Orval Watts.

31 Of 500,000 copies of *Roofs or Ceilings?* for distribution by the National Real Estate Association.

32 The paragraph reads: "The fact that, under free market conditions, better quarters go to those who have larger incomes or more wealth is, if anything, simply a reason for taking long-term measures to reduce the inequality of income and wealth. For those, like us, who would like even more equality than there is at present, not alone for housing but for all products, it is surely better to attack directly existing inequalities in income and wealth at the source than to ration each of the hundreds of commodities and services that compose our standard of living. It is the height of folly to permit individuals to receive unequal money incomes and then to take elaborate and costly measures to prevent them from using their incomes." *Roofs or Ceilings? The Current Housing Problem*, condensed for and issued by National Association of Real Estate Boards, Washington, D.C., 1946, p. 6.

33 Foundation for Economic Education.

34 Leonard E. Read.

35 *Saturday Evening Post.*

36 C. Pigou, London: Macmillan, 1945. Stigler's review was published in the *American Economic Review*, 36 (Dec. 1946): 927–8.

37 This reference is to an exchange of letters between V. Orval Watts, who wrote Stigler a lengthy letter dated August 28, 1946, and Stigler's reply to Watts dated September 3, 1946. Copies of those letters were apparently included with this letter of Stigler to Friedman.

38 Margaret "Chick" Stigler.

39 James W. Mack and Mabel Waller Mack.
40 Margaret Stigler was pregnant with Joseph.
41 Dean, School of Business, University of Rhode Island, then President Associated Colleges of Upper New York.
42 David Stigler.
43 Stephen M. Stigler.
44 National Association of Manufacturers.
45 V. Orval Watts.
46 Foundation for Economic Education.
47 F. A. Hayek.
48 David Ricardo.
49 For publication of both the expanded and condensed versions of *Roofs or Ceilings?*
50 Further along Stigler says that he has found the letter, but it is missing from the collection.
51 Of Stigler, *The Theory of Price*, Chicago: University of Chicago Press, 1946. The footnote reads:

> The principle of an increasing S_{yx} corresponds to the older theory of diminishing marginal utility of a commodity as its quantity increases. The two principles are equivalent in the special case where the marginal utility of X is independent of the quantity of Y; in general, however, neither necessarily implies the other.

52 Alfred Marshall, *Principles of Economics*, 8th edition, London: Macmillan, 1920.
53 The allusion is to Friedman's Ph.D. thesis, *Income From Independent Professional Practice*, with Simon Kuznets, New York: National Bureau of Economic Research, 1945.
54 The footnote to which Watts refers reads thus:

> Editor's note: The authors fail to state whether the "long-term measures" which they would adopt go beyond elimination of special privilege, such as monopoly now protected by government. In any case, however, the significance of their argument at this point deserves special notice. It means that, even from the standpoint of those who put equality above justice and liberty, rent controls are "the height of folly."
>
> *(Roofs or Ceilings?*, p. 10)

55 Friedman and Stigler did object. Friedman relates in his memoirs, "We were certainly justified in being outraged by what happened.... Without asking our permission, an anonymous "Editor's Note" ... was appended.... We both regarded this note, which in effect accused us of putting equality above justice and liberty, as inexcusable, and for some years we refused to have anything to do with the foundation or with Leonard Read." *Two Lucky People*, p. 151.
56 Stigler taught at both Brown and Columbia in the autumn 1946 term, commuting between his home in Providence, RI and his part-time position at Columbia.
57 Arthur F. Burns.
58 James W. Angell.
59 John M. Clark.

60   Carter Goodrich.
61   Robert M. Haig.
62   Stigler was one of two candidates for a permanent position at Columbia. Albert G. Hart was the other candidate for the position.
63   William J. Carson.
64   W. Allen Wallis.
65   William Vickery.
66   Alfred Marshall.
67   Charles E. Lindblom.
68   "The Economics of Minimum Wage Legislation," *American Economic Review*, 36 (June 1946), 358–65.
69   Moses Abramovitz.
70   Geoffrey H. Moore. Spelled "Geff" in original.
71   Leo Wolman.
72   Abraham Wald.
73   Abraham Wald, *Sequential Analysis*, New York: John Wiley & Sons, 1947.
74   The editors have been unable to discover who this Cisco is.
75   Draft of "Notes on the History of the Giffen Paradox."
76   Alfred Marshall.
77   Stigler took Friedman's advice and "Notes on the History of the Giffen Paradox," was published in the *Journal of Political Economy* 55 (April 1947): 152–6.
78   Stigler, *The Theory of Price*, 1946.
79   S_{yx} is the marginal rate of substitution of Y for X, "the amount of Y necessary to offset the loss of one (small) unit of X." Stigler, *The Theory of Price*, 1946, p. 70.
80   Enclosure missing.
81   Edward S. Shaw, "Elements of a Theory of Inventory," *Journal of Political Economy* 48 (August 1940): 465–86.
82   Joseph Stigler.
83   Arthur F. Burns.
84   Albert G. Hart.
85   In fact, Hart was offered the position at Columbia which he accepted.
86   Columbia created an additional position for Stigler who accepted it.
87   Paul A. Samuelson.
88   Paul H. Douglas.
89   Samuelson decided to remain at M.I.T.
90   Frank H. Knight.
91   Lloyd W. Mints.
92   H. Gregg Lewis.
93   To attend the American Economic Association meeting in Atlantic City, NJ, January 23–26, 1947.
94   This reference is to the University of Chicago's 4-E faculty contract.
95   The next U.S. recession began in November 1948 and ended in October 1949.
96   Arthur F. Burns.
97   Frederick C. Mills.
98   "Lange on Price Flexibility and Employment," *American Economic Review* 36 (September 1946): 613–31.

99 Most likely William J. Carson, Executive Director, National Bureau of Economic Research.
100 Joseph Stigler.
101 "Lerner on the Economics of Control," *Journal of Political Economy* 55 (October 1947): 405–16.
102 Abba P. Lerner.
103 Friedman's musings on the relative effects of income and excise taxes resulted in "The 'Welfare' Effects of an Income Tax and an Excise Tax," *Journal of Political Economy* 60 (February 1952): 25–33.
104 *Income from Independent Professional Practice*, with Simon Kuznets, New York: National Bureau of Economic Research, 1945.
105 Fritz Machlup.
106 Richard A. Lester.
107 Lester wrote "Marginalism, Minimum Wages, and Labor Markets," *American Economic Review*, 37 (March, 1947) 135–48 as a rejoinder to Machlup, "Marginal Analysis and Empirical Research," *American Economic Review*, 36 (Sept. 1946): 519–54 and as a critique of Stigler, "The Economics of Minimum Wage Legislation," *American Economic Review* 36 (June 1946): 358–65. Lester's article was followed by two rejoinders: Machlup, "Rejoinder to an Antimarginalist," *American Economic Review* 37 (March 1947): 148–54 and Stigler, "Professor Lester and the Marginalists," *American Economic Review* 37 (March 1947): 154–7.
108 Margaret Stigler.
109 Enclosure One.
110 Enclosure is missing.
111 Frederick A. Hayek.
112 Arthur L. Bowley (1869–1957) was Professor of Economic Statistics, London School of Economics and University of London. His work on English budget studies (R. G. D. Allen and A. Bowley, *Family Expenditure*. London: P. S. King, 1935) is cited as empirical evidence against the Giffen Paradox in Stigler's "Notes on the History of the Giffen Paradox."
113 Rockefeller Foundation.
114 Aaron Director.
115 The foundational meeting of the Mont Pelerin Society took place April 1–10, 1947 near Vevey, Switzerland. It was organized by Frederick Hayek and participants included George Stigler, Milton Friedman, and Milton Friedman's brother-in-law, University of Chicago Professor of Law, Aaron Director (1901–2004). Also attending were Leonard Read and V. Orval Watts of the Foundation for Economic Education.
116 Stephen M. Stigler.
117 Joseph Stigler.
118 Margaret Stigler.
119 Theodore W. Schultz.
120 Stigler may be referring to Anne Wallis, wife of W. Allan Wallis.
121 Leonard Jimmie Savage and Jane Kretschmer Savage.
122 Paul A. Samuelson.
123 Lloyd A. Metzler.
124 See Friedman, *Price Theory: A Provisional Text*, revised edition, Chicago: Aldine, 1962, p. 268.

125 Friedman and Stigler were both planning to attend the inaugural Mont Pelerin Society meeting, due to start in Switzerland April 1, 1947.
126 Richard L. Kozelka.
127 Charles E. Lindblom.
128 Max F. Millikan.
129 Lloyd A. Metzler.
130 Draft of "Lerner on the Economics of Control."
131 "Lange on Price Flexibility and Employment."
132 Arthur F. Burns.
133 Simon S. Kuznets.
134 The editors have been unable to discover who this Cisco is.
135 Francis M. Boddy. Stigler, Boddy, and Frederic B. Garver were coauthors of *Materials for Advanced General Economics*, St. Louis: Swift, 1939.
136 Paul T. Homan, Editor of the *American Economic Review*.
137 Edwin G. Nourse, Chairman, Council of Economic Advisers.
138 "Lerner on the Economics of Control," *Journal of Political Economy* 55 (October 1947): 405–16. The draft with Stigler's holographic notations is in the Milton Friedman Papers.
139 E. H. Chamberlin, "Review of *The Theory of Price* by G. Stigler," *American Economic Review* 37 (June 1947): 414–18.
140 Paul T. Homan, Editor of the *American Economic Review*.
141 "shudder" in original.
142 "A Monetary and Fiscal Framework for Economic Stability," *American Economic Review* 38 (June 1948): 245–64. Friedman presented an earlier version to the Econometric Society, September 17, 1947.
143 This is likely a draft of "Monopolistic Competition in Retrospect," in *Five Lectures on Economic Problems*, London, New York: Longmans, Green: New York: Macmillan, 1950; Freeport, NY: Books for Libraries, 1969.
144 Friedrich Lutz, Harry D. Gideonse, and Maurice Allais.
145 Robert M. Hutchins, University of Chicago President, 1929–45, Chancellor, 1945–51.
146 Thomas J. Watson, Jr.
147 Arthur F. Burns.
148 Of the National Bureau of Economic Research.
149 L. J. Savage, "Samuelson's Foundations: Its Mathematics," *Journal of Political Economy* 56 (June 1948): 200–2.
150 "Monopolistic Competition in Retrospect," in *Five Lectures on Economic Problems*, London, New York: Longmans, Green: New York: Macmillan, 1950; Freeport, NY: Books for Libraries, 1969. Friedman misspelled Chamberlin as Chamberlain.
151 "Review of *Monopolistic Competition and General Equilibrium Theory*," by Robert Triffin. *Journal of Farm Economics* 23 (February 1941): 389–90.
152 "Monopolistic Competition in Retrospect," in *Five Lectures on Economic Problems*, London, New York: Longmans, Green: New York: Macmillan, 1950; Freeport, NY: Books for Libraries, 1969.
153 Joseph H. Willits, Rockefeller Foundation. In the letter to Arthur Burns (November 24, 1947) Stigler proposed a research study of factual errors in articles published in major economics journals.
154 William Vickery.
155 Alfred G. Hart.

156 Simon Kuznets.
157 Carl Shoup.
158 Alvin H. Hansen, "Cost Functions and Full Employment," 37 (September 1947): 552–65.
159 Seymour E. Harris, "Some Aspects of the Wage Problem," 29 (August 1947): 145–53.
160 Robert L. Bishop, "Professor Knight and the Theory of Demand," 54 (April 1946): 141–69.
161 See Stigler, "Monopolistic Competition in Retrospect," in *Five Lectures on Economic Problems*, London, New York: Longmans, Green: New York: Macmillan, 1950; Freeport, NY: Books for Libraries, 1969.
162 This discussion may be based on Friedman's reading of Stigler, *The Theory of Price*, ch. 8.
163 Office of Price Administration.
164 Securities and Exchange Commission.
165 Joseph L. McConnell, "Corporate Earnings by Size of Firm," *Survey of Current Business*, May 1945 and "1942 Profits by Size of Firm," *Survey of Current Business*, January 1946.
166 Colin Clark.
167 Arthur Burns.
168 Simon Kuznets.
169 Cowles Commission.
170 Philip Young.
171 *New York Times*
172 American Economic Association meeting, December 28–31, 1947.
173 Stephen M. Stigler.
174 "The Division of Labor Is Limited by the Extent of the Market," *Journal of Political Economy* 59 (June 1951): 185–93.
175 Stigler, "The Kinky Oligopoly Demand Curve and Rigid Prices," *Journal of Political Economy* 55 (October 1947): 432–49.
176 Stigler, "A Theory of Delivered Price Systems," *American Economic Review* 39 (December 1949): 1143–59.
177 Jacob Viner, Arthur Smithies.
178 American Economic Association meeting, December 28–31, 1947.
179 Rose Friedman.
180 Neither the enclosure mentioned here nor that mentioned in the next paragraph is filed with the letter in the Friedman Papers.
181 National Bureau of Economic Research.
182 Paul H. Douglas and H. Gregg Lewis, *Studies on Consumer Expenditures*, Chicago: University of Chicago Press, 1947.
183 In *Five Lectures on Economic Problems*, London, New York: Longmans, Green, 1949: New York: Macmillan, 1950. This paper may be one of the enclosures with Stigler's December 15, 1947 letter.
184 The reference is to Stigler's March 1948 lectures at the University of London.
185 At the University of London. See *Five Lectures on Economic Problems*, London, New York: Longmans, Green, 1949: New York: Macmillan, 1950.
186 John Jewkes, *Ordeal by Planning*, London and New York: Macmillan, 1948; Reviewed by R. F. Harrod, *Economica*, New Series, 15: 59 (August 1948): 221–4.
187 This was likely part of the University of Chicago Free Market Study.

188 Howard S. Ellis.
189 Lloyd W. Mints.
190 F. A. Hayek.
191 Charles O. Hardy.
192 Friedrich A. Lutz.
193 Fritz Machlup.
194 Arthur Smithies.
195 National Bureau of Economic Research.
196 A University of Chicago faculty contract.
197 Moses Abramovitz.
198 W. Allen Wallis.
199 Lorie Tarshis. Stigler did not publish this.
200 Margaret Stigler.
201 Arthur F. Burns.
202 The editors have been unable to identify this award.
203 The University of Chicago Round Table, an NBC radio program.
204 "The Marshallian Demand Curve," *Journal of Political Economy* 57 (December 1949): 463–95. Reprinted in *Essays in Positive Economics*, Chicago, IL: University of Chicago Press, 1953.
205 F. Y. Edgeworth.
206 A. C. Pigou, S. J. Chapman.
207 "Stigler's Law," a typescript of which is in the Friedman Papers. In this unpublished paper Stigler presents empirical and a priori demonstrations that "all demand curves are inelastic, and all supply curves as inelastic too."
208 J. K. Galbraith and Arthur Smithies.
209 P. A. Samuelson.
210 University of Buffalo.
211 The editors have found no record of Stigler being at Princeton.
212 M. A. Abramovitz, "Monopolistic Selling in a Changing Economy," *Quarterly Journal of Economics* 52 (February 1938): 191–214.
213 "Monopoly and Oligopoly by Merger," *American Economic Review* 40 (May 1950): 23–34.
214 *Principles of Economics*, London: Macmillan, 1890.
215 "The Marshallian Demand Curve," *Journal of Political Economy* 57 (December 1949): 463–95. Reprinted in *Essays in Positive Economics*, Chicago, IL: University of Chicago Press, 1953.
216 A. A. Cournot.
217 Bureau of Labor Statistics.
218 *Employment and Compensation in Education*, New York: National Bureau of Economic Research, 1950.
219 H. H. Gossen and A. J. E. J. Dupuit. See "The Development of Utility Theory," *Journal of Political Economy* 58 (August 1950): 307–27 and (October): 373–96.
220 *The Theory of Price*, revised edition, New York: Macmillan, 1952.
221 W. C. Mitchell, *Lecture Notes on Types of Economic Theory, as Delivered by Wesley C. Mitchell*. New York: A. M. Kelley, 1949.
222 A. A. Cournot.
223 The author is most likely W. D. Grampp. The article was not published. However see his "Discussion," (in *The Housing Problem: I. The Current Situation*) *American Economic Review* 41 (May 1951): 583–5.

224   *Employment and Compensation in Education*, New York: National Bureau of Economic Research, 1950.

225   H. H. Gossen.

226   "The Utility Analysis of Choices Involving Risk," with L. J. Savage, *Journal of Political Economy* 56 (August 1948): 270–304.

227   "Demand Curves," in R. H. I. Palgrave, *Dictionary of Political Economy*, vol. 1, London: Macmillan, 1894.

228   *The Pure Theory of Foreign Trade. The Pure Theory of Domestic Values.* London: London School of Economics and Political Science, 1930.

229   *Memorials of Alfred Marshall.* Edited by A. C. Pigou. London: Macmillan, 1925.

230   "Descriptive Validity vs. Analytical Relevance in Economic Theory," mimeo, summer 1948 (draft of "The Methodology of Positive Economics" in *Essays in Positive Economics*, Chicago: University of Chicago Press, 1953).

231   "Monopolistic Competition in Retrospect," in *Five Lectures on Economic Problems*, London, New York: Longmans, Green, 1949; New York: Macmillan, 1950.

232   F. A. Fetter.

233   Geoffrey H. Moore

234   "The Utility Analysis of Choices Involving Risk," with L. J. Savage, *Journal of Political Economy* 56 (August 1948): 270–304.

235   *Employment and Compensation in Education*, New York: National Bureau of Economic Research, 1950.

236   Draft of "The Marshallian Demand Curve."

237   "Descriptive Validity vs. Analytical Relevance in Economic Theory," mimeo, summer 1948 (draft of "The Methodology of Positive Economics," in *Essays in Positive Economics*, Chicago: University of Chicago Press, 1953).

238   Leo Wolman.

239   F. A. Hayek.

240   Institute for Advanced Study.

241   Arthur F. Burns.

242   *Trends in Employment in the Service Industries*, Princeton, NJ: Princeton University Press for the National Bureau of Economic Research, 1956.

243   National Bureau of Economic Research.

244   Falk Foundation.

245   "Monopoly and Oligopoly by Merger," *American Economic Review* 40 (May 1950): 23–34.

246   "A Theory of Delivered Price Systems," *American Economic Review* 39 (December 1949): 1143–59.

247   "The Problem of Economic Stability," with E. Despres, A. G. Hart, P. A. Samuelson, and D. H. Wallace, *American Economic Review* 40 (September 1950): 505–38.

248   "Wesley C. Mitchell as an Economic Theorist," *Journal of Political Economy* 58 (December 1950): 465–93.

249   W. C. Mitchell, New York and London: McGraw-Hill, 1937.

250   See W. C. Mitchell to J. M. Clark, August 9, 1928, reprinted in Stuart A. Rice, *Methods in Social Science: A Case Book*, pp. 675–80, Chicago: University of Chicago Press, 1931.

251   "A Monetary and Fiscal Framework for Economic Stability," *American Economic Review* 38 (June 1948): 245–64.

252   "The Economics of Minimum Wage Legislation," *American Economic Review* 36 (June 1946): 358–65.

253   Wesley C. Mitchell died October 29, 1948. A memorial meeting was held for him in the Rotunda of Low Memorial Library, Columbia University, on December 4, 1948.

254   See J. A. Schumpeter, "Wesley Clair Mitchell (1874–1948)" *Quarterly Journal of Economics* 64 (February 1950): 139–55.

255   National Bureau of Economic Research.

256   Aaron Director.

257   C. O. Hardy, revised edition, Chicago: University of Chicago Press, 1931.

258   F. A. Fetter, *The Masquerade of Monopoly*, New York: Harcourt Brace, 1931.

259   J. A. Schumpeter.

260   P. A. Samuelson chaired a session on "Liquidity and Uncertainty" at the 1948 American Economic Association meeting in Cleveland, OH. Friedman was among the discussants of papers by A. G. Hart and Jacob Marschak.

261   "Dynamic Process Analysis," in H. S. Ellis, ed., *A Survey of Contemporary Economics*, pp. 352–87, Homewood, IL: Richard D. Irwin, Inc., 1948.

262   "The Simple Mathematics of Income Determination," in L. A. Metzler, ed., *Income, Employment and Public Policy: Essays in Honor of Alvin Hansen*, New York: Norton, 1948.

263   "Consumption Theory in Terms of Revealed Preference," *Economica*, New Series, 15 (November 1948): 243–53.

264   Herman O. A. Wold, "Synthesis of Pure Demand Analysis," I-III, *Skandinavisk Aktuarietidskrift*, 1943–44.

265   *Economics*, New York: McGraw-Hill, 1948.

266   K. E. Boulding and G. S. Stigler, eds., *Readings in Price Theory*, Homewood, IL: Richard D. Irwin, Inc., 1952.

267   K. E. Boulding and G. S. Stigler, eds, *Readings in Price Theory*, Homewood, IL: Richard D. Irwin, Inc., 1952.

268   O. Lange.

269   P. Wicksteed, London: Routledge, [1910] 1933.

270   "The Development of Utility Theory," (2 pts). *Journal of Political Economy* 58 (August 1950): 307–27; (October 1950): 373–96.

271   W. C. Mitchell, "Bentham's Felicific Calculus," *Political Science Quarterly* 33 (June 1918): 161–83.

272   Lionel Robbins, *A History of Economic Thought: The LSE Lectures*, edited by Steven G. Medema and Warren J. Samuels, Princeton, NJ: Princeton University Press, 1998.

273   Knut Wicksell, *Lectures on Political Economy*, volume 1, translated from Swedish by E. Classen and edited by L. Robbins, London: Routledge & Kegan Paul, Ltd, 1934.

274   J. A. Schumpeter, "Irving Fisher's Econometrics," *Econometrica* 16 (July 1948): 219–31.

275   Janet Friedman.

276   "Wesley C. Mitchell as an Economic Theorist," *Journal of Political Economy* 58 (December 1950): 465–93.

277   W. C. Mitchell, *Business Cycles*, Berkeley: University of California Press, 1913.

278   E. F. Heckscher, *Mercantilism*, London: G. Allen & Unwin, 1935.

279   *Lecture Notes on Types of Economic Theory, as Delivered by Wesley C. Mitchell*, New York: A. M. Kelley, 1949.

280 *History of the Greenbacks*, Chicago, IL: University of Chicago Press, 1903; *Gold, Prices, and Wages Under the Greenback Standard*, Berkeley, CA: The University Press, 1908.
281 T. R. Malthus.
282 A. H. Hansen.
283 D. H. Robertson.
284 *Principles of Economics*, London: Macmillan, 1895.
285 1920.
286 "The Development of Utility Theory," (2 pts). *Journal of Political Economy* 58 (August 1950): 307–27; (October 1950): 373–96.
287 "The Development of Utility Theory," (2 pts). *Journal of Political Economy* 58 (August 1950): 307–27; (October 1950): 373–96.
288 "The Marshallian Demand Curve," *Journal of Political Economy* 57 (December 1949): 463–95.
289 Marshall, *Principles of Economics*, London: Macmillan, 1890 and 1920.
290 C. R. Noyes.
291 *Employment and Compensation in Education*, New York: National Bureau of Economic Research, 1950.
292 A. F. Burns.
293 G. H. Moore.
294 United Nations, *National and International Measures for Full Employment, Report by [John Maurice Clark and others] a Group of Experts Appointed by the Secretary-General*, Lake Success, NY: UN Department of Economic Affairs, 1949.
295 F. A. Lutz.
296 N. W. Senior, W. F. Lloyd, R. Jennings.
297 E. J. Hamilton.
298 R. D. Friedman, "Bibliography of Articles on Price Theory," in G. S. Stigler and K. E. Boulding, eds, *Readings in Price Theory*, Homewood, IL: Richard D. Irwin, 1952.
299 Blakiston Company, publishers.
300 B. F. Haley.
301 F. M. Boddy.
302 "The Development of Utility Theory," (2 pts). *Journal of Political Economy*58 (August 1950): 307–27; (October 1950): 373–96.
303 Economic Cooperation Administration. The reference may be to Donald J. Dewey, "Crisis in Britain: A Note on the Stagnation Thesis," *Journal of Political Economy* 59 (August 1951): 348:52.
304 "The Development of Utility Theory. II," *Journal of Political Economy* 58 (October 1950): 373–96.
305 Arthur F. Burns.
306 This may be either *New Facts on Business Cycles*, New York: National Bureau of Economic Research, May 1950, or *Wesley Mitchell and the National Bureau*, New York: National Bureau of Economic Research, May 1949.
307 Eugen Slutsky.
308 Paul T. Homan.
309 Jacob Marschak.
310 A. N. Komolgoroff and V. I. Smirnov.
311 David Ricardo, *Principles of Political Economy and Taxation*, London: J. M.

158 *Notes*

Dent & Sons and New York: E. P. Dutton & Co., 1933; see George J.
Stigler, "The Ricardian Theory of Value and Distribution," *Journal of Political Economy* 60 (June 1952): 187–207.

312 *Principles of Economics*, London: Macmillan, 1890.
313 *The Pure Theory of Foreign Trade. The Pure Theory of Domestic Values*,
Privately printed. Reprinted in 1930, London: London School of Economics,
Scarce Works in Economics No. 1, 1879.
314 F. H. Knight, "Realism and Relevance in the Theory of Demand," *Journal of
Political Economy* 52 (December 1944): 289–318 and M. Friedman, "The
Marshallian Demand Curve," *Journal of Political Economy* 57 (December
1949): 463–95.
315 "The Marshallian Demand Curve," *Journal of Political Economy* 57
(December 1949): 463–95.
316 Stigler, *The Theory of Price*, New York: Macmillan, 1947, pp. 81–2; Friedman, "The 'Welfare' Effects of an Income and an Excise Tax," *Journal of
Political Economy* 60 (February 1952): 25–33.
317 "The Marshallian Demand Curve," *Journal of Political Economy* 57
(December 1949): 463–95.
318 Edward Levi.
319 R. D. Friedman, "Bibliography of Articles on Price Theory," in G. S. Stigler
and K. E. Boulding, eds, *Readings in Price Theory*, Homewood, IL: Richard
D. Irwin, 1952.
320 "The Development of Utility Theory," (2 pts). *Journal of Political Economy*
58 (August 1950): 307–27; (October 1950): 373–96.
321 "The Marshallian Demand Curve," *Journal of Political Economy* 57
(December 1949): 463–95.
322 E. J. Hamilton, editor of the *Journal of Political Economy*.
323 Friedman and L. J. Savage, "The Utility Analysis of Choices Involving
Risk," *Journal of Political Economy* 56 (August 1948): 270–304.
324 K. E. Boulding.
325 Moses Abramovitz, "Monopolistic Selling in a Changing Economy," *Quarterly Journal of Economics* 52 (February 1938): 191–214. They did not
include the article.
326 "Two Statements on Monopoly," Hearings Before the Subcommittee on the
Study of Monopoly Power, House of Representatives, Committee on Judi-
ciary, Apr 18–May 11, 1950.
327 Paul T. Homan, Managing Editor of the *American Economic Review*.
328 F. H. Knight. Knight was President of the American Economic Association
and program chair for the 1950 AEA meeting, December 27–30, Chicago,
IL.
329 D. Gale Johnson gave a paper "Rent Control and the Distribution of Income"
(*American Economic Review* 41 (May 1951): 569–82) in a session on "The
Housing Problem."
330 In the autumn of 1950 Friedman worked in Paris in the Finance and Trade
Division of the Office of the Special Representative for Europe, US Economic Cooperation Administration. The letter is on ECA stationary.
331 Lionel Robbins.
332 Arthur F. Burns.
333 G. J. Stigler and K. E. Boulding, eds, *Readings in Price Theory*, Homewood,
IL: Richard D. Irwin, 1952.

334   L. J. Savage.
335   Sarah Landau Friedman.
336   "The Case for Flexible Exchange Rates," in *Essays in Positive Economics*, Chicago, IL: University of Chicago Press, 1953, had its origins in a memorandum Friedman wrote for the Economic Cooperation Administration.
337   Arthur F. Burns.
338   Lionel Robbins.
339   Robert M. Hutchins served as President and Chancellor of the University of Chicago from 1929 until 1951.
340   *Business Concentration and Price Policy*, Princeton, NJ: Princeton University Press for the National Bureau of Economic Research, 1955.
341   Friedman and Savage rewrote a statement of formal properties of their utility function for probabilistic outcomes after Paul Samuelson pointed out an error in the statement as originally written. See *Readings in Price Theory*, p. 71, n. 24.
342   This may be "The Division of Labor is Limited by the Extent of the Market," *Journal of Political Economy* 59 (June 1951): 185–93.
343   Arthur F. Burns.
344   National Bureau of Economic Research.
345   Arthur F. Burns; Frederick C. Mills.
346   Theodore W. Schultz. Schultz gave the extension and enhanced the offer to what Stigler described to James Angell as "very generous terms," a salary of $14,000 for a 4Q contract or $14,500 for a 4E contract. Stigler remained at Columbia.
347   Arthur F. Burns.
348   "The 'Welfare' Effects of an Income Tax and an Excise Tax," *Journal of Political Economy* 60 (February 1952): 25–33.
349   "The Marshallian Demand Curve," *Journal of Political Economy* 57 (December 1949): 463–95.
350   "The Ricardian Theory of Value and Distribution," *Journal of Political Economy* 60 (June 1952): 187–207.
351   Friedrich and Helene Hayek.
352   Theodore and Esther Schultz.
353   "The Ricardian Theory of Value and Distribution," *Journal of Political Economy* 60 (June 1952): 187–207.
354   Earl Hamilton.
355   *An Essay on the Principle of Population*, London: J. Johnson, 1798.
356   Sir Edward West, *The Application of Capital to Land*, 1815, reprinted with an introduction by J. H. Hollander, Baltimore, MD: The Lord Baltimore Press, 1903.
357   L. I. Dublin and A. J. Lotka, New York: Ronald, 1930.
358   H. Kneeland, *Consumer Expenditures in the United States*, Washington D.C.: Government Printing Office, 1939.
359   "The Relevance of Economic Analysis to Prediction and Policy," mimeo [fall 1952]. This was a draft of "The Methodology of Positive Economics," in *Essays in Positive Economics*, Chicago, IL: University of Chicago Press, 1953.
360   "Sraffa's Ricardo," *American Economic Review* 43 (September 1953): 586–99.
361   Friedman was a Fulbright fellow at Cambridge University in 1953–54.
362   Columbia University celebrated its 200th anniversary in 1954.
363   Lionel Robbins, Dennis Robertson, W. A. Lewis, Wilhelm Roepke.
364   David Friedman.

365   National Bureau of Economic Research.

366   Arthur F. Burns, Soloman Fabricant.

367   Simon Kuznets.

368   Raymond Goldsmith, Ruth P. Mack, and G. Warren Nutter. See G. W. Nutter, "Measuring Production in the USSR: Industrial Growth in the Soviet Union," *American Economic Review* 48 (May 1958): 398–411.

369   Ford Foundation.

370   The enclosed are three pages of comments on a manuscript preliminary to *A Theory of the Consumption Function*, Princeton, NJ: Princeton University Press for the National Bureau of Economic Research, 1957.

371   "Some Questions About Growth Economics," *American Economic Review* 44 (March 1954): 53–63.

372   "An Evaluation of Freely-Fluctuating Exchange Rates," Ph.D. dissertation, Columbia University, 1952.

373   "The Economies of Scale," *Journal of Law and Economics* 1 (October 1958): 54–71.

374   Annual meeting of the American Economic Association, Detroit, MI, December 28–30, 1954.

375   Stigler spent a sabbatical in Switzerland in 1955.

376   Albert Hunold.

377   John Van Sickle.

378   Draft of "Perfect Competition, Historically Contemplated," *Journal of Political Economy* 65 (February 1957): 1–17.

379   Aaron Director.

380   "Discussion of 'Report of the Attorney General's Committee on Antitrust Policy'," *American Economic Review* 46 (May 1956): 504–7.

381   Arthur F. Burns.

382   Center for Advanced Studies in the Behavioral Sciences, Stanford, CA.

383   American Economic Association, Cleveland, OH, December 27–29, 1956.

384   Review of Leo Rogin, *The Meaning and Validity of Economic Theory*, *American Economic Review* 47 (March 1957): 159–64.

385   "The Economies of Scale," *Journal of Law and Economics* 1 (October 1958): 54–71.

386   Harold Barger.

387   "The Relative Stability of Monetary Velocity and the Investment Multiplier in the United States, 1897–1958," with David Meiselman, in *Stabilization Policies*, pp. 165–268. Englewood Cliffs, NJ: Prentice-Hall, Inc., 1963.

388   *A Theory of the Consumption Function*, Princeton, NJ: Princeton University Press for the National Bureau of Economic Research, 1957.

389   "The Tenable Range of Functions of Local Government," in *Federal Expenditure Policies for Economic Growth and Stability*. 85th Congress, 1st session Joint Economic Committee. November 5, 1957.

390   W. Allen Wallis.

391   Center for Advanced Study of the Behavioral Sciences.

392   National Bureau of Economic Research.

393   Ralph W. Tyler.

394   W. Allen Wallis.

395   "The Tenable Range of Functions of Local Government," in *Federal Expenditure Policies for Economic Growth and Stability*. 85th Congress, 1st session Joint Economic Committee. November 5, 1957.

Index